ALL THAT FALL AND OTHER

Everett Frost is Professor of Radio, Television and Film at New York University. He is Producer/Director of *The Beckett Festival of Radio Plays* (1986–9) – the American national broadcast premieres of all the extant radio plays of Samuel Beckett, produced in consultation with Beckett, and co-author of the annotated catalogue of Beckett's *Notes Diverse Holo[graph]* manuscripts at Trinity College Dublin.

Titles in the Samuel Beckett series

ENDGAME
Preface by Rónán McDonald
COMPANY/ILL SEEN ILL SAID/WORSTWARD HO/STIRRINGS STILL
Edited by Dirk Van Hulle
KRAPP'S LAST TAPE AND OTHER SHORTER PLAYS
Preface by S. E. Gontarski
MURPHY
Edited by J. C. C. Mays
WATT
Edited by C. J. Ackerley
ALL THAT FALL AND OTHER PLAYS FOR RADIO AND SCREEN
Preface and Notes by Everett Frost
MOLLOY
Edited by Shane Weller
HOW IT IS
Edited by Magessa O'Reilly
THE EXPELLED/THE CALMATIVE/THE END/FIRST LOVE
Edited by Christopher Ricks
SELECTED POEMS 1930–1989
Edited by David Wheatley

Forthcoming titles

WAITING FOR GODOT
Preface by Mary Bryden
MORE PRICKS THAN KICKS
Edited by Cassandra Nelson
MALONE DIES
Edited by Peter Boxall
THE UNNAMABLE
Edited by Steven Connor
HAPPY DAYS
Preface by James Knowlson
TEXTS FOR NOTHING/RESIDUA/FIZZLES: SHORTER FICTION 1950–1981
Edited by Mark Nixon
MERCIER AND CAMIER
Edited by Sean Kennedy

SAMUEL BECKETT

All That Fall

and other plays for radio and screen

Preface and Notes by Everett Frost

ff

faber and faber

This edition first published in 2009
by Faber and Faber Ltd
Bloomsbury House
74–77 Great Russell Street
London WC1B 3DA

Typeset by RefineCatch Limited, Bungay, Suffolk
Printed in England by CPI Bookmarque, Croydon

A CIP record for this book
is available from the British Library

ISBN 978-0-571-24375-4

2 4 6 8 10 9 7 5 3 1

Contents

Preface vii
A Note on the Texts and Acknowledgements xxv
Table of Dates xxvii

Radio
    All That Fall 1
    Embers 33
    Rough for Radio I 49
    Rough for Radio II 57
    Words and Music 71
    Cascando 83

Film
    Film 95

Television
    Eh Joe 111
    Ghost Trio 121
    . . . but the clouds . . . 133
    Quad 141
    Nacht und Träume 147

Appendix One
    The Old Tune 153

Appendix Two
    Notes on Publication and Broadcast of Individual Plays 169

Preface

The success of *En attendant Godot* (*Waiting for Godot*) in Paris in January 1953 brought Samuel Beckett significant opportunities to write for radio, television and film. Nearly half of his shorter plays were written for these media and gathering them into a single volume acknowledges their notable place in his oeuvre. Beckett was to make major innovations in his works for radio and screen by declining to take for granted prevailing conventions or pre-conceptions concerning them, or to capitulate to popular appeal when writing for mass media. This left him free to explore their specific characteristics, such as the absence of visuals in radio, the presence of the camera in film, or the voyeuristic qualities of the television screen. Moreover, these works not only enter into dialogue with the media for which they were written, but with each other, and with Beckett's stage plays and fiction.

Radio

There had been prologues to Beckett's radio plays. In the immediate aftermath of the Second World War, he had volunteered for service in the Irish Red Cross hospital built in the heavily bombed Normandy town of Saint-Lô, and in 1946 submitted an account of his experiences entitled 'The Capital of the Ruins' to Radio Telefís Éireann (although it was not aired). A condensed version of *En attendant Godot* was broadcast on French radio on 17 February 1952 as part of the efforts of Roget Blin, its first producer and director, to get the play staged. Beckett's long and mutually rewarding connection with the BBC did not begin with drama, but with the reading of an

vii

excerpt from his novel *Watt* (1953) on the Third Programme on 7 September 1955.

In the late 1940s and throughout the 1950s radio drama was enjoying a post-war renaissance. The BBC sought out promising younger artists, commissioned radio adaptations of plays written for theatrical performance, and, above all, encouraged writing plays specifically for the radio medium. After Dylan Thomas's *Under Milkwood* (broadcast on 25 January 1954), the BBC was looking for a success, while the more entrepreneurial radio producers were also looking for an opportunity to embrace the *avant garde*. Beckett satisfied both criteria. In 1955 the BBC seriously considered a radio production of *En attendant Godot* (and commissioned the author to translate it into *Waiting for Godot*), but decided that the problems of making so visual a work intelligible in an aural medium were formidable, and encouraged Beckett to write a play specifically for radio instead. (Their prudence was warranted: when the BBC later broadcast a radio adaptation of *Waiting for Godot* (27 April 1960), it satisfied neither author nor director.)

Though initially cautious about writing for the new medium, Beckett warmed to the prospect, remarking in a letter to Nancy Cunard (4 July 1956): 'Am told [BBC Controller Val] Gielgud wants a play for 3rd programme. Never thought about radio play technique but in the dead of t'other night got a nice gruesome idea full of cartwheels and dragging of feet and puffing and panting which may or may not lead to something.'[1] What it led to, in addition to much-needed income, was *All That Fall*, broadcast on 13 January 1957, and the beginnings of a life-long collaboration with the BBC.

In some respects *All That Fall* seems conventional enough. We encounter Maddy Rooney – in her seventies, overweight and unwell – laboriously making her way to and then from the Boghill railroad station (the only named location in any Beckett play), whose many features are drawn from the Foxrock of Beckett's youth. The circumstantiality of detail and the particularity of stock characters suggest that Beckett was conjuring for radio an Irish village much as Dylan Thomas had conjured a Welsh one. But it is a very Beckettian conjuring, and anticipates his later exploration of the power of radio to locate the drama inside the head of the protagonist, evincing mental processes more directly than any other dramatic medium is able to do. Verbalising such interiorities is, perhaps, among the most compelling and perennial concerns of Beckett's work. In *All That Fall* we hear the world from inside the mind of Maddy Rooney, not as if we were 'there', but as it might be experienced by a woman 'in a state of abortive explosiveness', as Beckett once described Maddy to Billie Whitelaw.

After the success of *All That Fall* the BBC was eager for a sequel, but it was two years before Beckett provided one in the form of *Embers*, completed in February 1959. In the interim, the BBC broadcast an early version of *From an Abandoned Work* (spoken by Patrick Magee, 14 December 1957), billed by the Third Programme as 'A meditation by Samuel Beckett'. And, while this prose work was finding a home on radio, a tape recorder – such as the one on which Beckett had listened to a playback of *All That Fall* – was being incorporated into *Krapp's Last Tape*, the stage play that originated as a 'Magee Monologue' in part because Beckett had been so struck with Magee's radio voice.

Although he had serious reservations about *Embers*, Beckett confided to his American publisher Barney Rosset that it represented an 'attempt to write *for* the radio medium, rather than simply exploit the medium's technical possibilities'.[2] It explores ambiguities that exist only on radio. Thus Ada makes 'no sound as she sits', unlike Henry who does. Beckett once observed to Ludovic Janvier that '*Embers* depends upon an ambiguity: does the protagonist have a hallucination or is he in the presence of reality? A visual production would destroy the ambiguity.'[3] Such 'teasers' pervade the later theatrical and media works.

Beckett's next contribution to radio was not an original work but an adaptation of one by Robert Pinget, whom he had met through his French publisher, Jérôme Lindon, and whom he came to regard as among the most promising young writers in Paris. The two collaborated in 1957 and 1959 on the French translations of *All That Fall* and *Embers*. Pinget's own radio play, *La Manivelle* (the crank or handle of a hand organ), was broadcast by the BBC in French on 27 July 1959, after which the BBC commissioned Beckett to translate it for broadcast in English. *The Old Tune*, Beckett's 'adaptation', translates Pinget's Parisians (Toupin and Pommard) into Dubliners (Cream and Gorman), and turns their colloquial Parisian French into a colourful Dublin *argot* that retrospectively inserts the play into a tradition of Irish theatre reminiscent of O'Casey or Synge. 'I tried to keep down Irishism but it kept breaking through. Couldn't get his rhythms and loose syntax any other way,' Beckett wrote to Barbara Bray, who directed the BBC production.[4] The famous translator and pungent dialogue have subsequently overtaken Pinget's original, and *The Old Tune* has been included in Beckett's *Collected Dramatic Works* since 1984. But when S. E. Gontarski revived it in 1986, Beckett admonished him to 'be sure Pinget gets full & visible credit. *The Old Tune* his vision not mine.'[5] And yet it resonates with other Beckett dramas, notably *Rough for Theatre I* with its two old men (which Beckett may have begun drafting as early as the mid-1950s), and with *Waiting for Godot*, where Didi and Gogo are similarly able to wind each other up with a mixture of reminiscence, bravado and bull. *The Old Tune* appears as an appendix in this volume – on the one hand neither fully Beckett in quite the same way as are the other works included; but on the other, not possible in this form from any other hand.

Two further radio plays were sketched out in French in the early 1960s but unpublished until the 1970s. Beckett considered *Rough for Radio I* (*Esquisse radiophonique*) to be a discarded attempt at what became *Cascando*, and he discouraged its production, describing it to Everett Frost in 1985 as 'unfinished and now unfinishable'. In 1976 he complied with urgings from the BBC for a new piece that could be included in a programme celebrating his seventieth birthday, by reaching into his proverbial trunk for *Pochade radiophonique*, a radio play dating from a somewhat speculative 'années 60?'[6] and translating it for the BBC as *Rough for Radio* (published here as *Rough for Radio II* – in order of composition, however, it probably precedes *Rough for Radio I*).

Beckett's last two radio plays (1961–2) were written – the first in English, the second in French – in collaboration with composers. His cousin, John Beckett, had provided continuity or 'travelling music' to accompany readings from the prose works, which led to a commission for author and composer to collaborate in creating what became *Words and Music*. Similarly, Beckett's friend, the composer Marcel Mihalovici, having previously collaborated with him in creating an opera from *La Dernière bande* (*Krapp's Last Tape*) had received a commission to write a work for French radio and asked Beckett to provide a text, resulting in *Cascando*. In both plays, Beckett relinquished his usual meticulous control, relying on the composer to create half of the drama and one of the major characters. And whenever the score varies, the play varies.

With *Words and Music* Beckett created a play so radiophonic that it can only be fully experienced aurally. Music is often used to personify (whether the villain in vaudeville, or Siegfried in Wagner) in order to build tension, supply moods, or create background. But prior to Beckett no radio drama had used the unseen medium's unique ability to represent music itself, or words themselves. For 'Bob' (the name given to music in *Words and Music*) is not merely the conductor, ensemble, and score that one experiences at a concert; he is also the process of creating the music that takes place in the mind of the composer, which can be conveyed but not portrayed. Similarly 'Joe', the name given to words, includes not only their utterance but also the mental act of shaping them. It is therefore impossible fully to stage the play other than on the radio because – as with *Cascando*, in which Opener 'invokes' a music character and a word character – the essence of the action depends upon its being non-visual.

Beckett described *Words and Music* to Grove Press as a

'text-music tandem', and remarked to Theodor Adorno that it parodied the age-old debate, as to whether one gets closer to the truth through words or music – and in which music finally prevails.[7] It is a debate that Beckett encountered as a young man in the philosophy of Arthur Schopenhauer, for whom music, not being language-dependent, is more universal and speaks directly to the emotions, thus at least momentarily releasing auditors from the endless strivings of the will. When words accompany music, 'they must of course occupy only an entirely subordinate position, and adapt themselves completely to it'.[8] In *Words and Music*, 'Music always wins,' as Beckett told Katherine Worth.[9]

Film

By the early 1960s Beckett had ceased to write radio plays (although BBC radio continued to produce readings from his poetry and prose, and adaptations of his stage plays), but he had become interested in television as a medium for the exploration of consciousness and perception, and had begun thinking of a teleplay that would feature Jack MacGowran. In the event he was temporarily diverted to *Film* by Barney Rosset's offer in February 1963 to fund and produce a thirty-minute film if Beckett would write an original screenplay. Rosset's offer would have been tempting to Beckett, who as a young man had read film journals and criticism, and developed an informed interest in the technical aspects of film-making. Seeking a suitable vocation, he had written in 1936 to the Russian film-maker Sergei Eisenstein enquiring after the prospect of studying cinematography with him for a year, but in the turbulence of the 1930s never received an answer. Beckett's only screenplay written for theatrical release, *Film*, brought him to the United States for the first and only time in July–August 1964, so that he could actively participate in its filming. Under the pressure of other commitments MacGowran withdrew at the last moment, and Buster Keaton was induced to take the role.

As described by the director, Alan Schneider, 'the script appeared in the spring of 1963 as a fairly baffling when not downright inscrutable six-page outline. Along with pages of addenda in Sam's inimitable informal style: explanatory notes, a philosophical supplement, modest production suggestions, a series of hand-drawn diagrams.[10] In *Film* as elsewhere, Beckett occasionally uses philosophical premises as imaginative starting points for structuring a work, without being particularly concerned about the usefulness of such ideas in explaining the world or the work. *Film* imagines an attempt to embrace non-existence according to the epistemology of the Irish philosopher George Berkeley (1685–1753), whose premise was that 'esse est percipi' – that to be (i.e. to exist) is to be perceived. Without such perception, one's existence is erased. In Berkeley's philosophy we are assured of our continued and continuous existence because we are perceived in the mind of God. In Beckett's film the 'O' – a figure who is held in existence as an *O*bjectified perception – seeks to erase himself by eluding perception.[11] While waiting its chance, 'E', the scrutinising *E*ye of the camera, occasionally tests or inadvertently crosses the 'angle of immunity' (45°), the angle at which one can no longer see oneself reflected in a mirror; hence – in any film shoot – an angle not to be transgressed by the camera in the presence of reflective surfaces, lest it film its own reflected image. So long as 'E' respects this angle, self-perception is kept at bay. The difficulty is that he cannot continue to exist and escape awareness of his own existence. These – the perceived and perceiving selves, 'one striving to see one striving not to be seen', as Beckett remarked[12] – are mirror images of each other and, indeed, at the climactic moment the audience discovers that like the camera, 'E', 'O' has but one eye, wearing a patch over the other.

In *Film* Beckett made full use of the camera as a character in its own right, similar to his use of light in *Play*, written the previous year. Thus the camera is not an anonymous and impersonal mechanism for the audience to observe a scene, but a lurking doppelgänger playing a role, with a will of its own, stalking its prey. As the probing eye of the audience it makes us voyeurs, complicitous in its agenda, and confronts the self with the intolerable (because ineradicable) fact of self-consciousness.

Television

After *Film*, Beckett returned to the thought of writing a television play for Jack MacGowran. In April–May 1965 he drafted *Eh Joe* (the name of the protagonist changing from 'Jack' to 'Joe' in first draft), submitting it unsolicited to the BBC's head of plays (and director of *Words and Music*), Michael Bakewell. Subsequently directing the German production himself, Beckett began his lifelong and productive relationship with Süddeutscher Rundfunk (SDR) in Stuttgart, with Dr Reinhard Müller-Freinfels, its Head of Television Drama, and with Jim Lewis, the American cameraman who would become indispensable in helping Beckett achieve the desired camera and lighting effects.

As with the stage plays *Footfalls*, *Rockaby* and *That Time*, and the teleplay *Ghost Trio*, *Eh Joe* makes use of schizophonia, separating image from sound source: we see a character but hear a voice unsynchronised with the moving lips. In *Ghost Trio* the precise nature of the relationship between the two is left even more enigmatic than it had been with *Eh Joe*. The use of a sound track in asynchronous counterpoint, so as to scrutinise mental processes, was explored by Eisenstein as part of his theory of film montage (which depended upon 'the pronounced non-coincidence of sound with visual images') – Beckett was well aware of Eisenstein's description in *Film Form* of ' "inner monologue" as a literary method of abolishing the distinction between subject and object'. In montage, moreover, 'the narrative, meaning, and impact of a film is conveyed through the cutting and juxtaposition of disparate shots', so that the film as such resides not in its several elements, but in the reassembling of them in the mind of the viewer. This theory 'applied equally to the introduction of both sound and colour in film production'.

Before the advent of digital high-definition, television's shadowy images tended to flatten out depth and lacked the sharpness and clarity needed for expansive shots or landscapes. Television was more adapted to close-ups, equipped for scrutinising the individual face with what Beckett called its 'savage eye'.[13] The small screen, unlike the big one, is watched from close up, in the privacy of one's home, rather than from a distance, in darkness, in an experience shared with others: 'It's a peek through a keyhole,' Beckett remarked after watching a playback of *Eh Joe*.[14]

Following cinematic convention, when the camera works from the side or behind it is a witness to the action, making the audience privy, as at the beginning of *Eh Joe*. When it fixes on the face and moves relentlessly in, it is an interrogation – which, as Beckett noted, is the visual component of the voice in the head[15] – penetrating the workings of the mind, with the audience's passive compliance. In *Eh Joe* and again in *Ghost Trio* Beckett stretches this tradition by making the voice female, though there is no reason why the internalised voice need be of the same gender as that of the auditor. Like the Henry of *Embers*, who has killed off the voice of his father and may be wearing his wife's down to extinction, Joe has killed the voices of his mother and father, and is trying to silence the accuser afflicting his solitude. But he cannot. As Beckett told an interviewer while directing the play: 'Only if she lives can he satisfy the wish to kill her. She is dead, but in him she lives. That is his passion: to kill the voices he cannot kill.'[16]

Beckett had used New York as an opportunity to learn more about film-making, but it was a medium in which neither writer nor director had previous practical experience, and the producer but little. In the autumn of 1966, after initial reservations, he agreed to collaborate on the filming of *Comédie* (*Play*) by Marin Karmitz, an experienced cineaste with an aesthetic sensibility consonant with Beckett's own. Thus the stage play which had contributed conceptually to the scenario of *Film* became a film in its turn, and in the process became an invaluable source for techniques and imagery that would emerge – and re-emerge – in Beckett's subsequent stage and teleplays.

Television was well-suited to Beckett's movement away from realism and towards minimalism or formalism – towards the disembodiment, disjuncture and interiorising of the narrative process that is evident in his later work. It afforded him new opportunities to portray the fragile and ephemeral nature of the individual human life, the nature of consciousness, and to explore mind-body questions which he had absorbed from his extensive readings in philosophy, psychology, and linguistics. In the early 1960s most television was still in 'black and white', which in fact meant shades of grey, and the fluorescent screen made figures seem disembodied and interiors ghostly. In *Ghost Trio*, Beckett consciously exploits this aspect – 'All grey. Shades of grey' – of the little screen, and he changed F's costume from a dark suit to a grey dressing gown – making him a phantom analogy to the grey room in which he is immersed.

Stage plays, variously directed and re-directed, are inevitably subject to change. But the television plays included the possibility that in their first productions, at least, they could be honed and re-recorded under Beckett's own direction or supervision until they reflected his intentions. So that the teleplays, whether inadvertently or by design, preserve the most concrete evidence we have of how Beckett himself wanted things done, and implicitly provide invaluable dramaturgic guidance for subsequent productions or film adaptations of his stage plays. In general the German productions would seem to be closer to Beckett's intentions because he was able to direct these himself, and because they were usually created immediately subsequent to his active participation in the BBC productions, allowing him to incorporate into the latter what he had learned from the former. Additionally, SDR provided more generous rehearsal time and technical support than could be afforded by the BBC.

Ghost Trio, . . .*but the clouds*. . ., *Nacht und Träume*, and *Quad* were each written as media-specific teleplays, the first three of which contain intensely personal experiences of remembered music or poetry; while the fourth integrates original music with image and movement, much as his final two radio plays had done with words and music. All four use the fluorescence of the small screen to create a kind of spectral poetry composed of image, lighting, movement, music and text, and (with the exception of *Quadrat I*) textures of grey. The first three extend what Beckett in 1968 had already adumbrated to Jack MacGowran as 'the old idea of a man waiting in a room seen first at normal remove then investigated in detail'[17] – familiar from *Eh Joe*, but having its roots in Beckett's fiction from *Murphy* onwards.

In *Ghost Trio* the music is wordless and we are closer to the Schopenhauerian realm of raw emotion. It is left unclear as to whether the music emanates from the mind of F or from the cassette-player at hand (or a combination of both). The teleplay kept its first title, 'Tryst', until a late stage of development before acquiring the title that links it more overtly with Beethoven's fifth piano trio, excerpts from which are audible at key moments. The original title may also have been abandoned in order not to encourage the cliché that F is eagerly hoping for the awaited encounter. Like M in . . .*but the clouds*. . . he may well be; but it is also possible that he is dreading it, like Joe in *Eh Joe*. When F looks up and smiles at the end of the play, there is no way of knowing whether he is consoled by the music (for the non-appearance of an awaited visitor) or is now free to lose himself in it without fear of further distraction. The final musical excerpt is from the second, more vigorous and emotionally triumphant theme of the Beethoven largo – the only time this theme appears in the play. The text as such of *Ghost Trio* is minimal. The set required is imparted in a diagram, which is elaborated upon in the script for Voice ('V') in the first part ('Pre-action') and in the second part ('Action'), where it is not clear whether or not 'F' hears 'V' and (almost always) moves according to the instructions given, or whether 'F' is describing the action. 'V' does not seem to be in control, since 'F' can move independently of her instruction or description.

Beckett wrote . . .*but the clouds*. . . for the BBC to accompany *Ghost Trio* and the filmed version of *Not I* on the programme produced to celebrate his seventieth birthday. The familiar solitary man ('M') in his 'little sanctum' now narrates his own, first-person, description (voice-over) of his actions and motivations as they are enacted by him ('M1') on a set in which there are no camera movements. The dramatic climax is achieved in a subversion of the convention of synchronised sound: the voice uttering the words of the poem is not that of the woman's image mouthing them (as one might expect in a sound film), but of the narrator telling the story he performs. In a deliberate inversion of the asynchronisation of voice and image found in *Eh Joe* and *Ghost Trio*, the beggar and the vision for which he has begged are fused in an epiphany. 'Poetry only love' had been the play's working title (condensed from 'Poetry was her only love'); the final title, . . .*but the clouds*. . ., derives from the concluding lines of Yeats's 'The Tower', in which the speaker wonders: 'Does the imagination dwell the most / Upon a woman won or a woman lost?' – a frequent theme in Beckett, and a testament to his regard for Yeats's poetry.

Directing his own work became for Beckett a continuation of the writing process, and the script a hypothesis tested in rehearsal, where considerable modifications of the original concept would occur. Thus Beckett's highly valued cameraman at SDR recalled (in 1987) that the camera moves in the German production of *Eh Joe* were more flexible than those so precisely specified in the published script: 'I simply cannot remember us spending much time with centimetres and metres, etc. . . . the voice dictated the starting and stopping of the camera, perhaps we felt that rigid adherence to strict measurement wasn't necessary – it wouldn't be the first time that Sam abandoned his usually very exacting instructions.'[18] Similarly in *Ghost Trio* and . . .*but the clouds*. . ., the durations specified for the shots are more fluid (and differ from each other) in the English and German productions than the precise timings indicated in the published texts.

Quad, a 'ballet for four people', was written for Süddeutscher Rundfunk and televised in 1981 as 'Quadrat 1 + 2', and directed by Beckett. It is performed by four hooded mimes, preferably 'as alike in build as possible', their arms tightly crossed as if 'they were resisting a cold wind'.[19] Each is identified with a colour and a percussion instrument. Each mime twice walks an identically prescribed geometric course, alternating one side of the square with a diagonal until all four sides have been traversed, returning to the corner from which she or he started. They enter and exit sequentially at prescribed intervals and each from a sequentially prescribed different corner, such that all four corners are represented and the number of players on stage twice increases from one to four and then decreases from four to one. The invisible centre of the square ('E') emerges as the most palpable presence haunting the drama: 'a supposed danger zone', according to one of Beckett's typescripts.[20] When two of the four players approach the centre at the same time they avoid collision by an abrupt leftward movement. But since this movement is also made by the first solo player when there is no collision to avoid, there is no indication that the players are aware of each other.[21]

A sequel to the original scenario emerged from the discovery that Beckett had overestimated the time required to perform it, and that the performance looked good even on the black and white studio monitors. Beckett – all of whose other teleplays specify black and white – was delighted, remarking that it is 100,000 years later, and added *Quadrat 2*, in which the 'feverish monotony' of the first part is replaced by the players re-traversing their courses one more time at a slower speed, in black and white, and without musical accompaniment other than the emphatic sound of their wearily shuffling footfalls. What seems in the beginning to be a whimsical piece of choreography becomes increasingly disconcerting – the kind of unrelieved repetition suggested by Dante's *Inferno* (which Beckett knew intimately).

The teleplay seems simple, but it is in fact very difficult to perform. Each *Quadrat* must be filmed in a single take since it cannot be edited: a mis-step by any of the performers or a glitch in the music requires that the entire piece be recorded again from the beginning. At times there are four percussion beats occurring simultaneously – one in synchronisation with each performer. In the Stuttgart production the performers wore headphones concealed under their hoods in order to keep time to their own beat.[22]

Finally, *Nacht und Träume* (*Night and Dreams*), like *Quad* and like *Act Without Words I* and *II*, is a play without spoken words – a telemime. Its title comes from a Schubert *Lied* (D 827), and Beckett specified: 'text of song of course in German and to be left so in eventual translations', along with the German title to the English text.[23] Nowhere is the presence of a serene romanticism in this supposed pessimistic ironist more palpable than in this gentle last teleplay, in which 'the helping hand' so longed for by Maddy Rooney in Beckett's first play for radio finally appears, gender uncertain: 'one of our numerous teasers', as Beckett is reported to have said.[24]

Adaphatrôce

As Beckett achieved celebrity he was besieged with requests for permission to adapt works from one medium to another. Since genre-specificity was intrinsic to the act of writing (and of collaborating on or directing a production), he came increasingly to resist such 'adaphatrôce', as he once punned it, often regretting instances in which he had relented and given permission. The issue was not primarily about whether or not one might achieve an aesthetically satisfactory result by adapting the work for another medium, but rather of not obliterating its media-specific intentionalities or contextualising 'teasers' that had been left disturbingly uncontextualised – for example, by moving elusively abstract works in the direction of a plausible realism and intelligibility. His polemical letter to Barney Rosset is often cited, amid all the complications of permission and refusal, as a defining statement of Beckett's views on such matters (quoted, for example, as the frontispiece to Clas

Zilliacus's *Beckett and Broadcasting*), and it bears reprinting in an edition such as this:

> *All That Fall* is a specifically radio play, or rather radio text, for voices, not bodies. I have already refused to have it 'staged' and cannot think of it in such terms. A perfectly straight reading before an audience seems to me just barely legitimate, though even on this score I have my doubts. But I am absolutely opposed to any form of adaptation with a view to its conversion into 'theatre.' It is no more theatre than *End-Game* is radio and to 'act' it is to kill it. Even the reduced visual dimension it will receive from the simplest and most static of readings [. . .] will be destructive of what-ever quality it may have and which depends on the whole thing's *coming out of the dark*. [. . .] frankly the thought of *All That Fall* on a stage, however discreetly, is intolerable to me. If another *radio* performance could be given in the States, it goes without saying that I'd be very pleased.
>
> Now for my sins I have to go on and say that I can't agree with the idea of *Act Without Words* as a film. It is not a film, not conceived in terms of cinema. If we can't keep our genres more or less distinct, or extricate them from the confusion that has them where they are, we might as well go home and lie down.
>
> [from a letter to Barney Rosset, 27 August 1957]

Most attempts to cross the boundaries of what Beckett calls 'genre' have proved disappointing. He approved a film adaptation by Robert Pinget of *Tous ceux qui tombent* (*All That Fall*) for broadcast on French television (25 January 1963), then regret-ted having done so. Seeing a BBC broadcast of *Waiting for Godot*, he remarked: 'My play wasn't written for this box; it was written for small men locked in a big space, whereas they are too big for this place'.[25] Yet there are also instances in which a media adaptation of a stage-play gave it a newly 'Beckettian' life in the medium to which it had been transposed. The Marin

Karmitz film of *Comédie* (*Play*) powerfully recreates the work as a film. Beckett himself wrote a three-page memorandum of 'Suggestions for a t.v. *Krapp*'. In the version with Patrick Magee, the intentness of the close-up on the small screen captures the poignancy with which Krapp is absorbed in re-hearing the story of the girl in the punt, for example, and over-comes the distance between audience and performer imposed by the stage. The iconic film of Billie Whitelaw in *Not I*, with the Auditor eliminated and the screen filled with the twisting, writhing Mouth, gives the play such a compelling televisual existence that Beckett included it in his BBC and German seventieth birthday broadcasts *Shades/Schatten*. 'For once,' notes James Knowlson, 'a transfer to another medium had worked brilliantly in its own terms'.[26]

Sometimes the process has worked both ways: in adapting the stage-play *What Where* for television, Beckett created what is in effect his last teleplay, and solved problems that had dissatisfied him in the play's original medium. Subsequently the television script was itself (re)adapted for the stage, creating *What Where II*.[27] In execution and atmosphere according with the 'bodies & movement eliminated / faces only' specified in his 1985 project notebook,[28] the teleplay and revised stage-play more closely resemble the film of *Comédie* or . . .*but the clouds*. . . than their own stage original. It seems appropriate that Beckett's final performative gesture would be to so fuse theatre and media in the evolution of a single work that they can no longer be extricated from each other.

Notes

1 Harry Ransom Research Center, University of Texas, Austin, MS 93.
2 John Pilling, *A Samuel Beckett Chronology* (Palgrave/Macmillan 2006), p. 142.
3 Ludovic Janvier, *Pour Samuel Beckett* (Paris: Éditions de Minuit 1966), 127n19.
4 Trinity College Dublin (TCD) MS 10948/58 n.d (November 1959). With the permission of The Board of Trinity College Dublin.

5 C. J. Ackerley and S. E. Gontarski, *The Faber Companion to Samuel Beckett* (London: Faber 2006), p. 420.

6 Clas Zilliacus, *Beckett and Broadcasting: A Study of the Works of Samuel Beckett for and in Radio and Television* (Abo: Abo Akademiae Aboensis, 52:2 1976), p. 9.

7 Ibid. p. 114.

8 Arthur Schopenhauer, *The World as Will and Representation*, Vol. II (New York: Dover 1966), p. 448.

9 Katherine Worth, 'Words for Music, Perhaps', in Bryden, ed. *Samuel Beckett and Music* (Oxford: Clarendon 1998), p. 16.

10 Alan Schneider, 'On Directing *Film*', in Samuel Beckett, *'Film': Complete Scenario, Illustrations, Production Shots* (New York: Grove 1969), p. 63.

11 A preliminary draft identifies the 'search of non-being in flight from extraneous perception culminating in inescapability of self perception' as 'the subject of the film' (University of Reading UofR MS 1227/7/6/1).

12 S. E. Gontarski, *The Intent of Undoing in Samuel Beckett's Texts* (Bloomington: University of Indiana Press 1985), p. 112.

13 Jim Lewis, 'Beckett et la caméra', *Revue d'Ésthétique* (numéro hors-série), 1986, p. 371.

14 Zilliacus, p. 191.

15 Ibid. p. 183.

16 Ibid. p. 187.

17 James Knowlson, *Damned to Fame: The Life of Samuel Beckett* (London: Bloomsbury 1996), p. 555.

18 Jonathan Kalb, *Beckett in Performance* (Cambridge: Cambridge University Press 1989), 256n25.

19 Martha Fehsenfeld, 'Beckett's Late Works: An Appraisal', *Modern Drama* XXV:3 (Sept. 1982), p. 360–1.

20 UofR MS 2199; Knowlson, p. 673.

21 'Should solo player avoid E?' 'Yes if centre dramatized taboo & this rather than avoidance of collision the motive when two or more.' (UoR MS 2100; quoted in Mary Bryden, '*QUAD*: Dancing Genders', *The Savage Eye/L'Oeil Fauve, Samuel Beckett Today/Aujourd'hui* No. 4 (1995), p. 111.

22 Knowlson, p. 673.

23 Beryl S. and John Fletcher, *A Student's Guide to the Plays of Samuel Beckett* (London: Faber 1978), p. 268.

24 Knowlson, p. 682.

25 Ibid. p. 488.

26 Ibid. p. 620.

27 *Faber Companion*, p. 640.

28 S. E. Gontarski, ed. *The Theatrical Notebooks of Samuel Beckett*. Vol. IV: *The Shorter Plays* (London: Faber 1999), p. 427.

A Note on the Texts

This volume prints the texts of the media plays as forwarded by Samuel Beckett to his English language publishers (Faber and Faber in London and/or Grove Press in New York – and John Calder, for *The Old Tune*). Written over a period of over thirty years, originating variously in French and English (and often directed in German), and with production rather than publication as their primary objective, the texts vary in style, format, and accidentals. As Beckett gained experience in directing his own work, his scripts, while meticulously plotted, became something to be further shaped in production and post-production. While we have made every effort silently to correct minor flaws appearing in earlier editions, no attempt has been made to impose a rigorous consistency upon such diverse materials. Thus, for example, dimensions are given in feet for an American production of *Film*, but in metres for British/German television productions (sometimes abbreviated, sometimes not). Beckett's first radio play gives a formal cast list, while subsequent plays may or may not variously list characters or give an initial ('V', 'M') to indicate a voice or presence. It is possible that sometimes the word 'Cast' is deliberately omitted so as to avoid implying the actual or physical 'thereness' of ghostly presences who, like Ada in *Embers* or the Voice in *Eh Joe*, in Beckett's illimitable phrase, 'may not be quite all there'. In *Film*, the conveyance for O's photographs is variously referred to as a 'briefcase' and a 'case', and we have left such things alone.

More substantively, playscripts arrived at their publishers at various moments in their evolution: sometimes before production (in response to the publisher's request to have the text published at the time of broadcast), sometimes after production and incorporating modifications, or after production in one language and before production in another. Modifications made in French or German productions may or may not have been included in subsequent English editions (or incorporated into the British text but not the American – or vice-versa). For purposes of this edition, such labyrinths are noted incidentally but remain untrodden. That effort must necessarily await the multilingual variorum scholarly editions that will one day come, though not soon. In the interim the diligent reader is referred (for *Eh Joe* and *What Where*) to volume 4 of *The Theatrical Notebooks of Samuel Beckett: The Shorter Plays* (ed. S. E. Gontarski, Faber and Faber, 1999); to other editions noted in the footnotes; to the manuscript studies appearing in *The Journal of Beckett Studies* and *Samuel Beckett Today/Aujourd'hui*; and to those monographs and collections of essays devoted to Beckett's media plays.

Acknowledgements

I am grateful to my wife and fellow Beckett sojourner, Anna McMullan, for getting some of the wind out of my drafts.

Table of Dates

Where unspecified, translations from French to English or vice versa are by Beckett.

1906

13 April   Samuel Beckett [Samuel Barclay Beckett] born in 'Cooldrinagh', a house in Foxrock, a village south of Dublin, on Good Friday, the second child of William Beckett and May Beckett, née Roe; he is preceded by a brother, Frank Edward, born 26 July 1902.

1911

Enters kindergarten at Ida and Pauline Elsner's private academy in Leopardstown.

1915

Attends larger Earlsfort House School in Dublin.

1920

Follows Frank to Portora Royal, a distinguished Protestant boarding school in Enniskillen, County Fermanagh (soon to become part of Northern Ireland).

1923

October   Enrols at Trinity College Dublin (TCD) to study for an Arts degree.

1926

August   First visit to France, a month-long cycling tour of the Loire Valley.

1927

April–August   Travels through Florence and Venice, visiting museums, galleries, and churches.

December   Receives B.A. in Modern Languages (French and Italian) and graduates first in the First Class.

1928

Jan.–June	Teaches French and English at Campbell College, Belfast.
September	First trip to Germany to visit seventeen-year-old Peggy Sinclair, a cousin on his father's side, and her family in Kassel.
1 November	Arrives in Paris as an exchange *lecteur* at the École Normale Supérieure. Quickly becomes friends with his predecessor, Thomas McGreevy [after 1943, MacGreevy], who introduces Beckett to James Joyce and other influential anglophone writers and publishers.
December	Spends Christmas in Kassel (as also in 1929, 1930 and 1931).

1929

June	Publishes first critical essay ('Dante . . . Bruno . Vico . . Joyce') and first story ('Assumption') in *transition* magazine.

1930

July	*Whoroscope* (Paris: Hours Press).
October	Returns to TCD to begin a two-year appointment as lecturer in French.
November	Introduced by MacGreevy to the painter and writer Jack B. Yeats in Dublin.

1931

March	*Proust* (London: Chatto and Windus).
September	First Irish publication, the poem 'Alba' in *Dublin Magazine*.

1932

January	Resigns his lectureship via telegram from Kassel and moves to Paris.
Feb.–June	First serious attempt at a novel, the posthumously published *Dream of Fair to Middling Women*.
December	Story 'Dante and the Lobster' appears in *This Quarter* (Paris).

1933

3 May — Death of Peggy Sinclair from tuberculosis.

26 June — Death of William Beckett from a heart attack.

1934

January — Moves to London and begins psychoanalysis with Wilfred Bion at the Tavistock Clinic.

February — *Negro Anthology*, edited by Nancy Cunard and with numerous translations by Beckett from the French (London: Wishart and Company).

May — *More Pricks Than Kicks* (London: Chatto and Windus).

Aug.–Sept. — Contributes several stories and reviews to literary magazines in London and Dublin.

1935

November — *Echo's Bones and Other Precipitates*, a cycle of thirteen poems (Paris: Europa Press).

1936

Returns to Dublin.

29 September — Leaves Ireland for a seven-month stay in Germany.

1937

Apr.–Aug. — First serious attempt at a play, *Human Wishes*, about Samuel Johnson and his household.

October — Settles in Paris.

1938

6/7 January — Stabbed by a street pimp in Montparnasse. Among his visitors at Hôpital Broussais is Suzanne Deschevaux-Dumesnil, an acquaintance who is to become Beckett's companion for life.

March — *Murphy* (London: Routledge).

April — Begins writing poetry directly in French.

1939

3 September — Great Britain and France declare war on Germany. Beckett abruptly ends a visit to Ireland and returns to Paris the next day.

1940

June   Travels south with Suzanne following the Fall of France, as part of the exodus from the capital.

September   Returns to Paris.

1941

13 January   Death of James Joyce in Zurich.

1 September   Joins the Resistance cell Gloria SMH.

1942

16 August   Goes into hiding with Suzanne after the arrest of close friend Alfred Péron.

6 October   Arrival at Roussillon, a small village in unoccupied southern France.

1944

24 August   Liberation of Paris.

1945

30 March   Awarded the Croix de Guerre.

Aug.–Dec.   Volunteers as a storekeeper and interpreter with the Irish Red Cross in Saint-Lô, Normandy.

1946

July   Publishes first fiction in French – a truncated version of the short story 'Suite' (later to become 'La Fin') in *Les Temps modernes*, owing to a misunderstanding by editors – as well as a critical essay on Dutch painters Geer and Bram van Velde in *Cahiers d'art*.

1947

Jan.–Feb.   Writes first play, in French, *Eleutheria* (published posthumously).

April   *Murphy*, French translation (Paris: Bordas).

1948

                Undertakes a number of translations commissioned by UNESCO and by Georges Duthuit.

1950

25 August   Death of May Beckett.

1951

March   *Molloy*, in French (Paris: Les Éditions de Minuit).

November   *Malone meurt* (Paris: Minuit).

1952

     Purchases land at Ussy-sur-Marne, subsequently Beckett's preferred location for writing.

September   *En attendant Godot* (Paris: Minuit).

1953

5 January   Premiere of *Godot* at the Théâtre de Babylone in Montparnasse, directed by Roger Blin.

May   *L'Innommable* (Paris: Minuit).

August   *Watt*, in English (Paris: Olympia Press).

1954

8 September   *Waiting for Godot* (New York: Grove Press).

13 September   Death of Frank Beckett from lung cancer.

1955

March   *Molloy*, translated into English with Patrick Bowles (New York: Grove; Paris: Olympia).

3 August   First English production of *Godot* opens in London at the Arts Theatre.

November   *Nouvelles et Textes pour rien* (Paris: Minuit).

1956

3 January   American *Godot* premiere in Miami.

February   First British publication of *Waiting for Godot* (London: Faber).

October   *Malone Dies* (New York: Grove).

1957

January   First radio broadcast, *All That Fall* on the BBC Third Programme.

     Fin de partie, suivi de Acte sans paroles (Paris: Minuit).

28 March   Death of Jack B. Yeats.

August	*All That Fall* (London: Faber).
October	*Tous ceux qui tombent*, translation of *All That Fall* with Robert Pinget (Paris: Minuit).
1958	
April	*Endgame*, translation of *Fin de partie* (London: Faber).
	From an Abandoned Work (London: Faber).
July	*Krapp's Last Tape* in Grove Press's literary magazine, *Evergreen Review*.
September	*The Unnamable* (New York: Grove).
December	*Anthology of Mexican Poetry*, translated by Beckett (Bloomington: Indiana University Press; later reprinted in London by Thames and Hudson).
1959	
March	*La Dernière bande*, translation of *Krapp's Last Tape* with Pierre Leyris, in the Parisian literary magazine *Les Lettres nouvelles*.
2 July	Receives honorary D.Litt. degree from Trinity College Dublin.
November	*Embers* in *Evergreen Review*.
December	*Cendres*, translation of *Embers* with Pinget, in *Les Lettres nouvelles*.
	Three Novels: Molloy, Malone Dies, The Unnamable (New York: Grove; Paris: Olympia Press).
1961	
January	*Comment c'est* (Paris: Minuit).
24 March	Marries Suzanne at Folkestone, Kent.
May	Shares Prix International des Editeurs with Jorge Luis Borges.
August	*Poems in English* (London: Calder).
September	*Happy Days* (New York: Grove).
1963	
February	*Oh les beaux jours*, translation of *Happy Days* (Paris: Minuit).

May	Assists with the German production of *Play* (*Spiel*, translated by Elmar and Erika Tophoven) in Ulm.
22 May	Outline of *Film* sent to Grove Press. *Film* would be produced in 1964, starring Buster Keaton, and released at the Venice Film Festival the following year.

1964

March	*Play and Two Short Pieces for Radio* (London: Faber).
April	*How It Is*, translation of *Comment c'est* (London: Calder; New York: Grove).
June	*Comédie*, translation of *Play*, in *Les Lettres nouvelles*.
July–Aug.	First and only trip to the United States, to assist with the production of *Film* in New York.

1965

October	*Imagination morte imaginez* (Paris: Minuit).
November	*Imagination Dead Imagine* (London: *The Sunday Times*; Calder).

1966

January	*Comédie et Actes divers*, including *Dis Joe* and *Va et vient* (Paris: Minuit).
February	*Assez* (Paris: Minuit).
October	*Bing* (Paris: Minuit).

1967

February	*D'un ouvrage abandonné* (Paris: Minuit). *Têtes-mortes* (Paris: Minuit).
16 March	Death of Thomas MacGreevy.
June	*Eh Joe and Other Writings*, including *Act Without Words II* and *Film* (London: Faber).
July	*Come and Go*, English translation of *Va et vient* (London: Calder).
26 September	Directs first solo production, *Endspiel* (translation of *Endgame* by Elmar Tophoven) in Berlin.

November	*No's Knife: Collected Shorter Prose 1945–1966* (London: Calder).
December	*Stories and Texts for Nothing*, illustrated with six ink line drawings by Avigdor Arikha (New York: Grove).
1968	
March	*Poèmes* (Paris: Minuit).
December	*Watt*, translated into French with Ludovic and Agnès Janvier (Paris: Minuit).
1969	
23 October	Awarded the Nobel Prize for Literature. *Sans* (Paris: Minuit).
1970	
April	*Mercier et Camier* (Paris: Minuit). *Premier amour* (Paris: Minuit).
July	*Lessness*, translation of *Sans* (London: Calder).
September	*Le Dépeupleur* (Paris: Minuit).
1972	
January	*The Lost Ones*, translation of *Le Dépeupleur* (London: Calder; New York: Grove). *The North*, part of *The Lost Ones*, illustrated with etchings by Arikha (London: Enitharmon Press).
1973	
January	*Not I* (London: Faber).
July	*First Love* (London: Calder).
1974	
	Mercier and Camier (London: Calder).
1975	
Spring	Directs *Godot* in Berlin and *Pas moi* (translation of *Not I*) in Paris.
1976	
February	*Pour finir encore et autres foirades* (Paris: Minuit).
20 May	Directs Billie Whitelaw in *Footfalls*, which is performed with *That Time* at London's Royal

Court Theatre in honour of Beckett's
seventieth birthday.

Autumn   *All Strange Away*, illustrated with etchings by
Edward Gorey (New York: Gotham Book
Mart).

Foirades/Fizzles, in French and English,
illustrated with etchings by Jasper Johns (New
York: Petersburg Press).

December *Footfalls* (London: Faber).

1977
March   *Collected Poems in English and French* (London:
Calder; New York: Grove).

1978
May   *Pas*, translation of *Footfalls* (Paris: Minuit).
August   *Poèmes, suivi de mirlitonnades* (Paris: Minuit).

1980
January   *Compagnie* (Paris: Minuit).
Company (London: Calder).

May   Directs *Endgame* in London with Rick
Cluchey and the San Quentin Drama
Workshop.

1981
March   *Mal vu mal dit* (Paris: Minuit).
April   *Rockaby and Other Short Pieces* (New York:
Grove).
October   *Ill Seen Ill Said*, translation of *Mal vu mal dit*
(New York: *New Yorker*; Grove).

1983
April   *Worstward Ho* (London: Calder).
September *Disjecta: Miscellaneous Writings and a
Dramatic Fragment*, containing critical
essays on art and literature as well as the
unfinished play *Human Wishes*
(London: Calder).

1984
February Oversees San Quentin Drama Workshop

	production of *Godot*, directed by Walter Asmus, in London.
	Collected Shorter Plays (London: Faber; New York: Grove).
May	*Collected Poems 1930–1978* (London: Calder).
July	*Collected Shorter Prose 1945–1980* (London: Calder).
1989	
April	*Stirrings Still*, with illustrations by Louis le Brocquy (New York: Blue Moon Books).
June	*Nohow On: Company, Ill Seen Ill Said, Worstward Ho*, illustrated with etchings by Robert Ryman (New York: Limited Editions Club).
17 July	Death of Suzanne Beckett.
22 December	Death of Samuel Beckett. Burial in Cimetière de Montparnasse.

*

1990	
	As the Story Was Told: Uncollected and Late Prose (London: Calder; New York: Riverrun Press).
1992	
	Dream of Fair to Middling Women (Dublin: Black Cat Press).
1995	
	Eleutheria (Paris: Minuit).
1996	
	Eleutheria, translated into English by Barbara Wright (London: Faber).
1998	
	No Author Better Served: The Correspondence of Samuel Beckett and Alan Schneider, edited by Maurice Harmon (Cambridge MA: Harvard University Press).

2000

Beckett on Film: nineteen films, by different directors, of Beckett's works for the stage (RTÉ, Channel 4, and Irish Film Board; DVD, London: Clarence Pictures).

2006

Samuel Beckett: Works for Radio: The Original Broadcasts: five works spanning the period 1957–1976 (CD, London: British Library Board).

2009

The Letters of Samuel Beckett 1929–1940, edited by Martha Dow Fehsenfeld and Lois More Overbeck (Cambridge: Cambridge University Press).

Compiled by Cassandra Nelson

M1 ... M2 over table.
M2 ... in space

Man (M1 - bowed over table, M2 - in space)
Woman (W)
Man's voice (VM)
Woman's voice (VW)

come out - emerge?

sanctum - holy

1. ~~Crepuscular~~ Rhythm.

Between fade-outs + ups movement of ~~scene~~ shadow [dark]
e.g. 4. Fadeout on M. ~~shadow~~ [dark] 2" Fade up etc.
(same throughout).

Poetry was her only love.
W: Poetry (was my) only love.

Ghost Trio }
Poetry only love } ?
Not I

                                    N
                                Sanctum

            W   E
          Roads   Closet

                    A
            A Lit area
            B Standing position

Manuscript draft for . . . *but the clouds* . . .
Courtesy of the Beckett International Foundation, University of Reading.
© The Estate of Samuel Beckett.

All That Fall

A play for radio

Written in English in 1956. First broadcast on the BBC Third Programme on 13 January 1957. First published in 1957 by Grove Press (New York) and Faber and Faber.

CAST

MRS ROONEY (Maddy)	a lady in her seventies
CHRISTY	a carter
MR TYLER	a retired bill-broker
MR SLOCUM	Clerk of the Racecourse
TOMMY	a porter
MR BARRELL	a station-master
MISS FITT	a lady in her thirties
A FEMALE VOICE	
DOLLY	a small girl
MR ROONEY (Dan)	husband of Mrs Rooney, blind
JERRY	a small boy

Rural sounds. Sheep, bird, cow, cock, severally, then together. Silence.
MRS ROONEY *advances along country road towards railway station. Sound of her dragging feet.*
Music faint from house by way. "Death and the Maiden." The steps slow down, stop.

MRS ROONEY: Poor woman. All alone in that ruinous old house. [*Music louder. Silence but for music playing. The steps resume. Music dies.* MRS ROONEY *murmurs, melody. Her murmur dies. Sound of approaching cartwheels. The cart stops. The steps slow down, stop.*]
Is that you, Christy?

CHRISTY: It is, Ma'am.

MRS ROONEY: I thought the hinny was familiar. How is your poor wife?

CHRISTY: No better, Ma'am.

MRS ROONEY: Your daughter then?

CHRISTY: No worse, Ma'am.
[*Silence.*]

MRS ROONEY: Why do you halt? [*Pause.*] But why do I halt? [*Silence.*]

CHRISTY: Nice day for the races, Ma'am.

MRS ROONEY: No doubt it is. [*Pause.*] But will it hold up? [*Pause. With emotion.*] Will it hold up? [*Silence.*]

CHRISTY: I suppose you wouldn't—

MRS ROONEY: Hist! [*Pause*] Surely to goodness that cannot be the up mail I hear already.
[*Silence. The hinny neighs. Silence.*]

CHRISTY: Damn the mail.

3

MRS ROONEY: Oh thank God for that! I could have sworn I heard it, thundering up the track in the far distance. [*Pause.*] So hinnies whinny. Well, it is not surprising.

CHRISTY: I suppose you wouldn't be in need of a small load of dung?

MRS ROONEY: Dung? What class of dung?

CHRISTY: Stydung.

MRS ROONEY: Stydung . . . I like your frankness, Christy. [*Pause.*] I'll ask the master. [*Pause.*] Christy.

CHRISTY: Yes, Ma'am.

MRS ROONEY: Do you find anything . . . bizarre about my way of speaking? [*Pause.*] I do not mean the voice. [*Pause.*] No, I mean the words. [*Pause. More to herself.*] I use none but the simplest words, I hope, and yet I sometimes find my way of speaking very . . . bizarre. [*Pause.*] Mercy! What was that?

CHRISTY: Never mind her, Ma'am, she's very fresh in herself today.

[*Silence.*]

MRS ROONEY: Dung? What would we want with dung, at our time of life? [*Pause.*] Why are you on your feet down on the road? Why do you not climb up on the crest of your manure and let yourself be carried along? Is it that you have no head for heights?

[*Silence.*]

CHRISTY: [*To the hinny.*] Yep! [*Pause. Louder.*] Yep wiyya to hell owwa that!

[*Silence.*]

MRS ROONEY: She does not move a muscle. [*Pause.*] I too should be getting along, if I do not wish to arrive late at the station. [*Pause.*] But a moment ago she neighed and pawed the ground. And now she refuses to advance. Give her a good welt on the rump. [*Sound of welt. Pause.*] Harder! [*Sound of welt. Pause.*] Well! If someone were to do that for me I should not dally. [*Pause.*] How she gazes at me to be sure, with her great moist cleg-tormented eyes! Perhaps if I

4

were to move on, down the road, out of her field of vision
. . . [*Sound of welt.*] No, no, enough! Take her by the snaffle
and pull her eyes away from me. Oh this is awful! [*She
moves on. Sound of her dragging feet.*] What have I done to
deserve all this, what, what? [*Dragging feet.*] So long ago . . .
No! No! [*Dragging feet. Quotes.*] "Sigh out a something
something tale of things, Done long ago and ill done." [*She
halts.*] How can I go on, I cannot. Oh let me just flop down
flat on the road like a big fat jelly out of a bowl and never
move again! A great big slop thick with grit and dust and
flies, they would have to scoop me up with a shovel.
[*Pause.*] Heavens, there is that up mail again, what will
become of me! [*The dragging steps resume.*] Oh I am just a
hysterical old hag I know, destroyed with sorrow and pining
and gentility and churchgoing and fat and rheumatism and
childlessness. [*Pause. Brokenly.*] Minnie! Little Minnie!
[*Pause.*] Love, that is all I asked, a little love, daily, twice
daily, fifty years of twice daily love like a Paris horse-
butcher's regular, what normal woman wants affection? A
peck on the jaw at morning, near the ear, and another at
evening, peck, peck, till you grow whiskers on you. There is
that lovely laburnum again.
[*Dragging feet. Sound of bicycle-bell. It is old* MR TYLER
*coming up behind her on his bicycle, on his way to the station.
Squeak of brakes. He slows down and rides abreast of her.*]

MR TYLOR: Mrs Rooney! Pardon me if I do not doff my cap, I'd
fall off. Divine day for the meeting.

MRS ROONEY: Oh, Mr Tyler, you startled the life out of me
stealing up behind me like that like a deer-stalker! Oh!

MR TYLER: [*Playfully.*] I rang my bell, Mrs Rooney, the moment I
sighted you I started tinkling my bell, now don't you deny it.

MRS ROONEY: Your bell is one thing, Mr Tyler, and you are
another. What news of your poor daughter?

MR TYLER: Fair, fair. They removed everything, you know, the
whole . . . er . . . bag of tricks. Now I am grandchildless.
[*Dragging feet.*]

MRS ROONEY: Gracious how you wobble! Dismount, for mercy's sake, or ride on.

MR TYLER: Perhaps if I were to lay my hand lightly on your shoulder, Mrs Rooney, how would that be?
[*Pause.*] Would you permit that?

MRS ROONEY: No, Mr Rooney, Mr Tyler I mean, I am tired of light old hands on my shoulders and other senseless places, sick and tired of them. Heavens, here comes Connolly's van! [*She halts. Sound of motor-van. It approaches, passes with thunderous rattles, recedes.*] Are you all right, Mr Tyler? [*Pause.*] Where is he? [*Pause.*] Ah there you are! [*The dragging steps resume.*] That was a narrow squeak.

MR TYLER: I alit in the nick of time.

MRS ROONEY: It is suicide to be abroad. But what is it to be at home, Mr Tyler, what is it to be at home? A lingering dissolution. Now we are white with dust from head to foot. I beg your pardon?

MR TYLER: Nothing, Mrs Rooney, nothing I was merely cursing, under my breath, God and man, under my breath, and the wet Saturday afternoon of my conception. My back tyre has gone down again. I pumped it hard as iron before I set out. And now I am on the rim.

MRS ROONEY: Oh what a shame!

MR TYLER: Now if it were the front I should not so much mind. But the back. The back! The chain! The oil! The grease! The hub! The brakes! The gear! No! It is too much!
[*Dragging steps.*]

MRS ROONEY: Are we very late, Mr Tyler? I have not the courage to look at my watch.

MR TYLER: [*Bitterly.*] Late! I on my bicycle as I bowled along was already late. Now therefore we are doubly late, trebly, quadrupedly late. Would I had shot by you, without a word.
[*Dragging feet.*]

MRS ROONEY: Whom are you meeting, Mr Tyler?

6

MR TYLER: Hardy. [*Pause.*] We used to climb together. [*Pause.*] I saved his life once. [*Pause.*] I have not forgotten it. [*Dragging feet. They stop.*]

MRS ROONEY: Let us halt a moment and let this vile dust fall back upon the viler worms. [*Silence. Rural sounds.*]

MR TYLER: What sky! What light! Ah in spite of all it is a blessed thing to be alive in such weather, and out of hospital.

MRS ROONEY: Alive?

MR TYLER: Well half alive shall we say?

MRS ROONEY: Speak for yourself, Mr Tyler. I am not half alive nor anything approaching it. [*Pause.*] What are we standing here for? This dust will not settle in our time. And when it does some great roaring machine will come and whirl it all skyhigh again.

MR TYLER: Well, shall we be getting along in that case?

MRS ROONEY: No.

MR TYLER: Come, Mrs Rooney—

MRS ROONEY: Go, Mr Tyler, go on and leave me, listening to the cooing of the ringdoves. [*Cooing.*] If you see my poor blind Dan tell him I was on my way to meet him when it all came over me again, like a flood. Say to him, Your poor wife, She told me to tell you it all came flooding over her again and . . . [*The voice breaks.*] . . . she simply went back home . . . straight back home . . .

MR TYLER: Come, Mrs Rooney, come, the mail has not yet gone up, just take my free arm and we'll be there with time and to spare.

MRS ROONEY: [*Sobbing.*] What? What's all this now? [*Calmer.*] Can't you see I'm in trouble? [*With anger.*] Have you no respect for misery? [*Sobbing.*] Minnie! Little Minnie!

MR TYLER: Come, Mrs Rooney, come, the mail has not yet gone up, just take my free arm and we'll be there with time and to spare.

MRS ROONEY: [*Brokenly.*] In her forties now she'd be, I don't know, fifty, girding up her lovely little loins, getting ready for the change . . .

MR TYLER: Come, Mrs Rooney, come, the mail—

MRS ROONEY: [*exploding.*] Will you get along with you, Mr Rooney, Mr Tyler I mean, will you get along with you now and cease molesting me? What kind of a country is this where a woman can't weep her heart out on the highways and byways without being tormented by retired billbrokers! [*Mr Tyler prepares to mount his bicycle.*] Heavens you're not going to ride her flat! [*Mr Tyler mounts.*] You'll tear your tube to ribbons! [*Mr Tyler rides off. Receding sound of bumping bicycle. Silence. Cooing.*] Venus birds! Billing in the woods all the long summer long. [*Pause.*] Oh cursed corset! If I could let it out, without indecent exposure. Mr Tyler! Mr Tyler! Come back and unlace me behind the hedge! [*She laughs wildly, ceases.*] What's wrong with me, what's wrong with me, never tranquil, seething out of my dirty old pelt, out of my skull, oh to be in atoms, in atoms! [*Frenziedly.*] ATOMS! [*Silence. Cooing. Faintly.*] Jesus! [*Pause.*] Jesus!

[*Sound of car coming up behind her. It slows down and draws up beside her, engine running. It is* MR SLOCUM, *the Clerk of the Racecourse.*]

MR SLOCUM: Is anything wrong, Mrs Rooney? You are bent all double. Have you a pain in the stomach?

[*Silence.* MRS ROONEY *laughs wildly. Finally.*]

MRS ROONEY: Well if it isn't my old admirer the Clerk of the Course, in his limousine.

MR SLOCUM: May I offer you a lift, Mrs Rooney? Are you going in my direction?

MRS ROONEY: I am, Mr Slocum, we all are. [*Pause.*] How is your poor mother?

MR SLOCUM: Thank you, she is fairly comfortable. We manage to keep her out of pain. That is the great thing, Mrs Rooney, is it not?

MRS ROONEY: Yes, indeed, Mr Slocum, that is the great thing, I don't know how you do it. [*Pause. She slaps her cheek violently.*] Ah these wasps!

8

MR SLOCUM: [*Coolly.*] May I then offer you a seat, Madam?

MRS ROONEY: [*With exaggerated enthusiasm.*] Oh that would be heavenly, Mr Slocum, just simply heavenly. [*Dubiously.*] But would I ever get in? You look very high off the ground today, these new balloon tyres I presume. [*Sound of door opening and* MRS ROONEY *trying to get in.*] Does this roof never come off? No? [*Efforts of* MRS ROONEY.] No . . . I'll never do it . . . you'll have to get down, Mr Slocum, and help me from the rear. [*Pause.*] What was that? [*Pause. Aggrieved.*] This is all your suggestion, Mr Slocum, not mine. Drive on, Sir, drive on.

MR SLOCUM: [*Switching off engine.*] I'm coming, Mrs Rooney, I'm coming, give me time, I'm as stiff as yourself.

[*Sound of* MR SLOCUM *extracting himself from driver's seat.*]

MRS ROONEY: Stiff! Well I like that! And me heaving all over back and front. [*To herself.*] The dry old reprobate!

MR SLOCUM: [*In position behind her.*] Now, Mrs Rooney, how shall we do this?

MRS ROONEY: As if I were a bale, Mr Slocum, don't be afraid. [*Pause. Sounds of effort.*] That's the way! [*Effort.*] Lower! [*Effort.*] Wait! [*Pause.*] No, don't let go! [*Pause.*] Suppose I do get up, will I ever get down?

MR SLOCUM: [*Breathing hard.*] You'll get down, Mrs Rooney, you'll get down. We may not get you up, but I warrant you we'll get you down.

[*He resumes his efforts. Sound of these.*]

MRS ROONEY: Oh! . . . Lower! . . . Don't be afraid! . . . We're past the age when . . . There! . . . Now! . . . Get your shoulder under it . . . Oh! . . . [*Giggles.*] Oh glory! . . . Up! Up! . . . Ah! . . . I'm in! [*Panting of* MR SLOCUM. *He slams the door. In a scream.*] My frock! You've nipped my frock! [MR SLOCUM *opens the door.* MRS ROONEY *frees her frock.* MR SLOCUM *slams the door. His violent unintelligible muttering as he walks round to the other door. Tearfully.*] My nice frock! Look what you've done to my nice frock!

[MR SLOCUM *gets into his seat, slams driver's door, presses starter. The engine does not start. He releases starter.*] What will Dan say when he sees me?

MR SLOCUM: Has he then recovered his sight?

MRS ROONEY: No, I mean when he knows, what will he say when he feels the hole? [MR SLOCUM *presses starter. As before. Silence.*] What are you doing, Mr Slocum?

MR SLOCUM: Gazing straight before me, Mrs Rooney, through the windscreen, into the void.

MRS ROONEY: Start her up, I beseech you, and let us be off. This is awful!

MR SLOCUM: [*Dreamily.*] All morning she went like a dream and now she is dead. That is what you get for a good deed. [*Pause. Hopefully.*] Perhaps if I were to choke her. [*He does so, presses the starter. The engine roars. Roaring to make himself heard.*] She was getting too much air!

[*He throttles down, grinds in his first gear, moves off, changes up in a grinding of gears.*]

MRS ROONEY: [*In anguish.*] Mind the hen! [*Scream of brakes. Squawk of hen.*] Oh, mother, you have squashed her, drive on, drive on! [*The car accelerates. Pause.*] What a death! One minute picking happy at the dung, on the road, in the sun, with now and then a dust bath, and then—bang!—all her troubles over. [*Pause.*] All the laying and the hatching. [*Pause.*] Just one great squawk and then . . . peace. [*Pause.*] They would have slit her weasand in any case. [*Pause.*] Here we are, let me down. [*The car slows down, stops, engine running.* MR SLOCUM *blows his horn. Pause. Louder. Pause.*] What are you up to now, Mr Slocum? We are at a standstill, all danger is past and you blow your horn. Now if instead of blowing it now you had blown it at that unfortunate—

[*Horn violently.* TOMMY *the porter appears at top of station steps.*]

MR SLOCUM: [*Calling.*] Will you come down, Tommy, and help this lady out, she's stuck.

[TOMMY *descends the steps.*]

Open the door, Tommy, and ease her out.

[TOMMY *opens the door.*]

TOMMY: Certainly, Sir. Nice day for the races, Sir. What would you fancy for—

MRS ROONEY: Don't mind me. Don't take any notice of me. I do not exist. The fact is well known.

MR SLOCUM: Do as you're asked, Tommy, for the love of God.

TOMMY: Yessir. Now, Mrs Rooney.

[*He starts pulling her out.*]

MRS ROONEY: Wait, Tommy, wait now, don't bustle me, just let me wheel round and get my feet to the ground. [*Her efforts to achieve this.*] Now.

TOMMY: [*Pulling her out.*] Mind your feather, Ma'am.

[*Sounds of effort.*] Easy now, easy.

MRS ROONEY: Wait, for God's sake, you'll have me beheaded.

TOMMY: Crouch down, Mrs Rooney, crouch down, and get your head in the open.

MRS ROONEY: Crouch down! At my time of life! This is lunacy!

TOMMY: Press her down, Sir.

[*Sounds of combined efforts.*]

MRS ROONEY: Pity!

TOMMY: Now! She's coming! Straighten up, Ma'am! There!

[MR SLOCUM *slams the door.*]

MRS ROONEY: Am I out?

[*The voice of* MR BARRELL, *the station-master, raised in anger.*]

MR BARRELL: Tommy! Tommy! Where the hell is he?

[MR SLOCUM *grinds in his gear.*]

TOMMY: [*Hurriedly.*] You wouldn't have something for the Ladies Plate, Sir? I was given Flash Harry.

MR SLOCUM: [*Scornfully.*] Flash Harry! That carthorse!

MR BARRELL: [*At top of steps, roaring.*] Tommy! Blast your bleeding bloody— [*He sees* MRS ROONEY.] Oh, Mrs Rooney . . .
[MR SLOCUM *drives away in a grinding of gears.*] Who's that crucifying his gearbox, Tommy?

TOMMY: Old Cissy Slocum.

MRS ROONEY: Cissy Slocum! That's a nice way to refer to your betters. Cissy Slocum! And you an orphan!

MR BARRELL: [*Angrily to* TOMMY.] What are you doing stravaging down here on the public road? This is no place for you at all! Nip up there on the platform now and whip out the truck! Won't the twelve thirty be on top of us before we can turn round?

TOMMY: [*Bitterly.*] And that's the thanks you get for a Christian act.

MR BARRELL: [*Violently.*] Get on with you now before I report you! [*Slow feet of* TOMMY *climbing steps.*] Do you want me to come down to you with the shovel? [*The feet quicken, recede, cease.*] Ah God forgive me, it's a hard life. [*Pause.*] Well, Mrs Rooney, it's nice to see you up and about again. You were laid up there a long time.

MRS ROONEY: Not long enough, Mr Barrell. [*Pause.*] Would I were still in bed, Mr Barrell. [*Pause.*] Would I were lying stretched out in my comfortable bed, Mr Barrell, just wasting slowly, painlessly away, keeping up my strength with arrowroot and calves-foot jelly, till in the end you wouldn't see me under the blankets any more than a board. [*Pause.*] Oh no coughing or spitting or bleeding or vomiting, just drifting gently down into the higher life, and remembering, remembering . . . [*The voice breaks.*] . . . all the silly unhappiness . . . as though . . . it had never happened . . . What did I do with that handkerchief? [*Sound of handkerchief loudly applied.*] How long have you been master of this station now, Mr Barrell?

MR BARRELL: Don't ask me, Mrs Rooney, don't ask me.

MRS ROONEY: You stepped into your father's shoes, I believe, when he took them off.

MR BARRELL: Poor Pappy! [*Reverent pause.*] He didn't live long to enjoy his ease.

MRS ROONEY: I remember him clearly. A small ferrety purple-faced widower, deaf as a doornail, very testy and snappy.

[*Pause.*] I suppose you'll be retiring soon yourself, Mr Barrell, and growing your roses. [*Pause.*] Did I understand you to say the twelve thirty would soon be upon us?

MR BARRELL: Those were my words.

MRS ROONEY: But according to my watch which is more or less right—or was—by the eight o'clock news the time is now coming up to twelve . . . [*Pause as she consults her watch.*] . . . thirty-six. [*Pause.*] And yet upon the other hand the up mail has not yet gone through. [*Pause.*] Or has it sped by unbeknown to me? [*Pause.*] For there was a moment there, I remember now, I was so plunged in sorrow I wouldn't have heard a steam roller go over me. [*Pause.* MR BARRELL *turns to go.*] Don't go, Mr Barrell!

[MR BARRELL *goes. Loud.*] Mr Barrell! [*Pause. Louder.*] Mr Barrell! [MR BARRELL *comes back.*]

MR BARRELL: [*Testily.*] What is it, Mrs Rooney, I have my work to do.

[*Silence. Sound of wind.*]

MRS ROONEY: The wind is getting up. [*Pause. Wind.*] The best of the day is over. [*Pause. Wind. Dreamily.*] Soon the rain will begin to fall and go on falling, all afternoon. [MR BARRELL *goes.*] Then at evening the clouds will part, the setting sun will shine an instant, then sink, behind the hills. [*She realizes* MR BARRELL *has gone.*] Mr Barrell! Mr Barrell! [*Silence.*] I estrange them all. They come towards me, uninvited, bygones bygones, full of kindness, anxious to help . . . [*The voice breaks.*] . . . genuinely pleased . . . to see me again . . . looking so well . . . [*Handkerchief.*] A few simple words . . . from my heart . . . and I am all alone . . . once more . . . [*Handkerchief. Vehemently.*] I should not be out at all! I should never leave the grounds! [*Pause.*] Oh there is that Fitt woman, I wonder will she bow to me. [*Sound of* MISS FITT *approaching, humming a hymn. She starts climbing the steps.*] Miss Fitt! [MISS FITT *halts, stops humming.*] Am I then invisible, Miss Fitt? Is this cretonne so becoming to me that I merge into the masonry? [MISS

13

FITT *descends a step*.] That is right, Miss Fitt, look closely and you will finally distinguish a once female shape.

MISS FITT: Mrs Rooney! I saw you, but I did not know you.

MRS ROONEY: Last Sunday we worshipped together. We knelt side by side at the same altar. We drank from the same chalice. Have I so changed since then?

MISS FITT: [*Shocked.*] Oh but in church, Mrs Rooney, in church I am alone with my Maker. Are not you? [*Pause.*] Why even the sexton himself, you know, when he takes up the collection, knows it is useless to pause before me. I simply do not see the plate, or bag, whatever it is they use, how could I? [*Pause.*] Why even when all is over and I go out into the sweet fresh air, why even then for the first furlong or so I stumble in a kind of daze as you might say, oblivious to my co-religionists. And they are very kind I must admit—the vast majority—very kind and understanding. They know me now and take no umbrage. There she goes, they say, there goes the dark Miss Fitt, alone with her Maker, take no notice of her. And they step down off the path to avoid my running into them. [*Pause.*] Ah yes, I am distray, very distray, even on week-days. Ask Mother, if you do not believe me. Hetty, she says, when I start eating my doily instead of the thin bread and butter, Hetty, how can you be so distray? [*Sighs.*] I suppose the truth is I am not there, Mrs Rooney, just not really there at all. I see, hear, smell, and so on, I go through the usual motions, but my heart is not in it, Mrs Rooney, my heart is in none of it. Left to myself, with no one to check me, I would soon be flown . . . home. [*Pause.*] So if you think I cut you just now, Mrs Rooney, you do me an injustice. All I saw was a big pale blur, just another big pale blur. [*Pause.*] Is anything amiss, Mrs Rooney, you do not look normal somehow. So bowed and bent.

MRS ROONEY: [*Ruefully.*] Maddy Rooney, née Dunne, the big pale blur. [*Pause.*] You have piercing sight, Miss Fitt, if you only knew it, literally piercing. [*Pause.*]

MISS FITT: Well . . . is there anything I can do, now that I am here?

MRS ROONEY: If you would help me up the face of this cliff, Miss Fitt, I have little doubt your Maker would requite you, if no one else.

MISS FITT: Now, now, Mrs Rooney, don't put your teeth in me. Requite! I make these sacrifices for nothing—or not at all. [*Pause. Sound of her descending steps.*] I take it you want to lean on me, Mrs Rooney.

MRS ROONEY: I asked Mr Barrell to give me his arm, just give me his arm. [*Pause.*] He turned on his heel and strode away.

MISS FITT: Is it my arm you want then? [*Pause. Impatiently.*] Is it my arm you want, Mrs Rooney, or what is it?

MRS ROONEY: [*Exploding.*] Your arm! Any arm! A helping hand! For five seconds! Christ what a planet!

MISS FITT: Really . . . Do you know what it is, Mrs Rooney, I do not think it is wise of you to be going about at all.

MRS ROONEY: [*Violently.*] Come down here, Miss Fitt, and give me your arm, before I scream down the parish!

[*Pause. Wind. Sound of* MISS FITT *descending last steps.*]

MISS FITT: [*Resignedly.*] Well, I suppose it is the Protestant thing to do.

MRS ROONEY: Pismires do it for one another. [*Pause.*] I have seen slugs do it. [MISS FITT *proffers her arm.*] No, the other side, my dear, if it's all the same to you, I'm left-handed on top of everything else. [*She takes* MISS FITT'*s right arm.*] Heavens, child, you're just a bag of bones, you need building up. [*Sound of her toiling up steps on* MISS FITT'*s arm.*] This is worse than the Matterhorn, were you ever up the Matterhorn, Miss Fitt, great honeymoon resort. [*Sound of toiling.*] Why don't they have a handrail? [*Panting.*] Wait till I get some air. [*Pause.*] Don't let me go! [MISS FITT *hums her hymn. After a moment* MRS ROONEY *joins in with the words.*] . . . the encircling gloo-oom . . . [MISS FITT *stops humming.*] . . . tum tum me on. [*Forte.*] The night is dark and I am far from ho-ome, tum tum—

15

MISS FITT: [*Hysterically.*] Stop it, Mrs Rooney, stop it, or I'll drop you!

MRS ROONEY: Wasn't it that they sung on the *Lusitania*? Or Rock of Ages? Most touching it must have been. Or was it the *Titanic*?

[*Attracted by the noise a group, including* MR TYLER, MR BARRELL *and* TOMMY, *gathers at top of steps.*]

MR BARRELL: What the—
[*Silence.*]

MR TYLER: Lovely day for the fixture.

[*Loud titter from* TOMMY *cut short by* MR BARRELL *with backhanded blow in the stomach. Appropriate noise from* TOMMY.]

A FEMALE VOICE: [*Shrill.*] Oh look, Dolly, look!

DOLLY: What, Mamma?

A FEMALE VOICE: They are stuck! [*Cackling laugh.*] They are stuck!

MRS ROONEY: Now we are the laughing-stock of the twenty-six counties. Or is it thirty-six?

MR TYLER: That is a nice way to treat your defenceless subordinates, Mr Barrell, hitting them without warning in the pit of the stomach.

MISS FITT: Has anyone seen my mother?

MR BARRELL: Who is that?

TOMMY: The dark Miss Fitt.

MR BARRELL: Where is her face?

MRS ROONEY: Now, deary, I am ready if you are. [*They toil up remaining steps.*] Stand back, you cads! [*Shuffle of feet.*]

A FEMALE VOICE: Mind yourself, Dolly!

MRS ROONEY: Thank you, Miss Fitt, thank you, that will do, just prop me up against the wall like a roll of tarpaulin and that will be all, for the moment. [*Pause.*] I am sorry for all this ramdam, Miss Fitt, had I known you were looking for your mother I should not have importuned you, I know what it is.

MR TYLER: [*In marvelling aside.*] Ramdam!

A FEMALE VOICE: Come, Dolly darling, let us take up our stand before the first class smokers. Give me your hand and hold me tight, one can be sucked under.

MR TYLER: You have lost your mother, Miss Fitt?

MISS FITT: Good morning, Mr Tyler.

MR TYLER: Good morning, Miss Fitt.

MR BARRELL: Good morning, Miss Fitt.

MISS FITT: Good morning, Mr Barrell.

MR TYLER: You have lost your mother, Miss Fitt?

MISS FITT: She said she would be on the last train.

MRS ROONEY: Do not imagine, because I am silent, that I am not present, and alive, to all that is going on.

MR TYLER: [*To* MISS FITT.] When you say the last train—

MRS ROONEY: Do not flatter yourselves for one moment, because I hold aloof, that my sufferings have ceased. No. The entire scene, the hills, the plain, the racecourse with its miles and miles of white rails and three red stands, the pretty little wayside station, even you yourselves, yes, I mean it, and over all the clouding blue, I see it all, I stand here and see it all with eyes . . . [*The voice breaks.*] . . . through eyes . . . oh if you had my eyes . . . you would understand . . . the things they have seen . . . and not looked away . . . this is nothing . . . nothing . . . what did I do with that handkerchief? [*Pause.*]

MR TYLER: [*To* MISS FITT.] When you say the last train— [MRS ROONEY *blows her nose violently and long.*] —when you say the last train, Miss Fitt, I take it you mean the twelve thirty.

MISS FITT: What else could I mean, Mr Tyler, what else could I *conceivably* mean?

MR TYLER: Then you have no cause for anxiety, Miss Fitt, for the twelve thirty has not yet arrived. Look. [MISS FITT *looks.*] No, up the line. [MISS FITT *looks. Patiently.*] No, Miss Fitt, follow the direction of my index. [MISS FITT *looks.*] There. You see now. The signal. At the bawdy hour of nine. [*In rueful afterthought.*] Or three alas! [MR BARRELL *stifles a guffaw.*] Thank you, Mr Barrell.

MISS FITT: But the time is now getting on for—

MR TYLER: [*Patiently.*] We all know, Miss Fitt, we all know only too well what the time is now getting on for, and yet the cruel fact remains that the twelve thirty has not yet arrived.

MISS FITT: Not an accident, I trust! [*Pause.*] Do not tell me she has left the track! [*Pause.*] Oh darling mother! With the fresh sole for lunch!

[*Loud titter from* TOMMY, *checked as before by* MR BARRELL.]

MR BARRELL: That's enough old guff out of you. Nip up to the box now and see has Mr Case anything for me.

[TOMMY *goes.*]

MRS ROONEY: Poor Dan!

MISS FITT: [*In anguish.*] What terrible thing has happened?

MR TYLER: Now now, Miss Fitt, do not—

MRS ROONEY: [*With vehement sadness.*] Poor Dan!

MR TYLER: Now now, Miss Fitt, do not give way . . . to despair, all will come right . . . in the end. [*Aside to* MR BARRELL.] What *is* the situation, Mr Barrell? Not a collision surely?

MRS ROONEY: [*Enthusiastically.*] A collision! Oh that would be wonderful!

MISS FITT: [*Horrified.*] A collision! I knew it!

MR TYLER: Come, Miss Fitt, let us move a little up the platform.

MRS ROONEY: Yes, let us all do that. [*Pause.*] No? [*Pause.*] You have changed your mind? [*Pause.*] I quite agree, we are better here, in the shadow of the waiting-room.

MR BARRELL: Excuse me a moment.

MRS ROONEY: Before you slink away, Mr Barrell, please, a statement of some kind, I insist. Even the slowest train on this brief line is not ten minutes and more behind its scheduled time without good cause, one imagines. [*Pause.*] We all know your station is the best kept of the entire network, but there are times when that is not enough, just not enough. [*Pause.*] Now, Mr Barrell, leave off chewing your whiskers, we are waiting to hear from you—we the unfortunate ticket-holders' nearest if not dearest.

[*Pause.*]

MR TYLER: [*Reasonably.*] I do think we are owed some kind of explanation, Mr Barrell, if only to set our minds at rest.

MR BARRELL: I know nothing. All I know is there has been a hitch. All traffic is retarded.

MRS ROONEY: [*Derisively.*] Retarded! A hitch! Ah these celibates! Here we are eating our hearts out with anxiety for our loved ones and he calls that a hitch! Those of us like myself with heart and kidney trouble may collapse at any moment and he calls that a hitch! In our ovens the Saturday roast is burning to a shrivel and he calls that—

MR TYLER: Here comes Tommy, running! I am glad I have been spared to see this.

TOMMY: [*Excitedly, in the distance.*] She's coming. [*Pause. Nearer.*] She's at the level-crossing!
[*Immediately exaggerated station sounds. Falling signals. Bells. Whistles. Crescendo of train whistle approaching. Sound of train rushing through station.*]

MRS ROONEY: [*Above rush of train.*] The up mail! The up mail! [*The up mail recedes, the down train approaches, enters the station, pulls up with great hissing of steam and clashing of couplings. Noise of passengers descending, doors banging,* MR BARRELL *shouting "Boghill! Boghill!", etc. Piercingly.*] Dan! . . . Are you all right? . . . Where is he? . . . Dan! . . . Did you see my husband? . . . Dan! . . . [*Noise of station emptying. Guard's whistle. Train departing, receding. Silence.*] He isn't on it! The misery I have endured to get here, and he isn't on it! . . . Mr Barrell! . . . Was he not on it? [*Pause.*] Is anything the matter, you look as if you had seen a ghost. [*Pause.*] Tommy! . . . Did you see the master?

TOMMY: He'll be along, Ma'am, Jerry is minding him.
[MR ROONEY *suddenly appears on platform, advancing on small boy* JERRY's *arm. He is blind, thumps the ground with his stick and pants incessantly.*]

MRS ROONEY: Oh, Dan! There you are! [*Her dragging feet as she hastens towards him. She reaches him. They halt.*] Where in the world were you?

MR ROONEY: [*Coolly.*] Maddy.

MRS ROONEY: Where were you all this time?

MR ROONEY: In the men's.

MRS ROONEY: Kiss me!

MR ROONEY: Kiss you? In public? On the platform? Before the boy? Have you taken leave of your senses?

MRS ROONEY: Jerry wouldn't mind. Would you, Jerry?

JERRY: No, Ma'am.

MRS ROONEY: How is your poor father?

JERRY: They took him away, Ma'am.

MRS ROONEY: Then you are all alone?

JERRY: Yes, Ma'am.

MR ROONEY: Why are you here? You did not notify me.

MRS ROONEY: I wanted to give you a surprise. For your birthday.

MR ROONEY: My birthday?

MRS ROONEY: Don't you remember? I wished you your happy returns in the bathroom.

MR ROONEY: I did not hear you.

MRS ROONEY: But I gave you a tie! You have it on!

[*Pause.*]

MR ROONEY: How old am I now?

MRS ROONEY: Now never mind about that. Come.

MR ROONEY: Why did you not cancel the boy? Now we shall have to give him a penny.

MRS ROONEY: [*Miserably.*] I forgot! I had such a time getting here! Such horrid nasty people! [*Pause. Pleading.*] Be nice to me, Dan, be nice to me today!

MR ROONEY: Give the boy a penny.

MRS ROONEY: Here are two halfpennies, Jerry. Run along now and buy yourself a nice gobstopper.

JERRY: Yes, Ma'am.

MR ROONEY: Come for me on Monday, if I am still alive.

JERRY: Yessir.

[*He runs off.*]

MR ROONEY: We could have saved sixpence. We have saved fivepence. [*Pause.*] But at what cost?

[*They move off along platform arm in arm. Dragging feet, panting, thudding stick.*]

MRS ROONEY: Are you not well?

[*They halt, on* MR ROONEY's *initiative.*]

MR ROONEY: Once and for all, do not ask me to speak and move at the same time. I shall not say this in this life again.

[*They move off. Dragging feet, etc. They halt at top of steps.*]

MRS ROONEY: Are you not—

MR ROONEY: Let us get this precipice over.

MRS ROONEY: Put your arm around me.

MR ROONEY: Have you been drinking again? [*Pause.*] You are quivering like a blancmange. [*Pause.*] Are you in a condition to lead me? [*Pause.*] We shall fall into the ditch.

MRS ROONEY: Oh, Dan! It will be like old times!

MR ROONEY: Pull yourself together or I shall send Tommy for the cab. Then instead of having saved sixpence, no, fivepence, we shall have lost . . . [*Calculating mumble.*] . . . two and three less six one and no plus one one and no plus three one and nine and one ten and three two and one . . . [*Normal voice.*] two and one, we shall be the poorer to the tune of two and one. [*Pause.*] Curse that sun, it has gone in. What is the day doing?

[*Wind.*]

MRS ROONEY: Shrouding, shrouding, the best of it is past. [*Pause.*] Soon the first great drops will fall splashing in the dust.

MR ROONEY: And yet the glass was firm. [*Pause.*] Let us hasten home and sit before the fire. We shall draw the blinds. You will read to me. I think Effie is going to commit adultery with the Major. [*Brief drag of feet.*] Wait! [*Feet cease. Stick tapping at steps.*] I have been up and down these steps five thousand times and still I do not know how many there are. When I think there are six there are four or five or seven or eight and when I remember there are five there are three or four or six or seven and when finally I realize there are seven there are five or six or eight or nine. Sometimes I wonder if they do not change them in the night. [*Pause. Irritably.*] Well? How many do you make them today?

MRS ROONEY: Do not ask me to count, Dan, not now.

MR ROONEY: Not count! One of the few satisfactions in life!

MRS ROONEY: Not steps, Dan, please, I always get them wrong. Then you might fall on your wound and I would have that on my manure-heap on top of everything else. No, just cling to me and all will be well.

[*Confused noise of their descent. Panting, stumbling, ejaculations, curses. Silence.*]

MR ROONEY: Well! That is what you call well!

MRS ROONEY: We are down. And little the worse. [*Silence. A donkey brays. Silence.*] That was a true donkey. Its father and mother were donkeys.

[*Silence.*]

MR ROONEY: Do you know what it is, I think I shall retire.

MRS ROONEY: [*Appalled.*] Retire! And live at home? On your grant!

MR ROONEY: Never tread these cursed steps again. Trudge this hellish road for the last time. Sit at home on the remnants of my bottom counting the hours—till the next meal. [*Pause.*] The very thought puts life in me! Forward, before it dies!

[*They move on. Dragging feet, panting, thudding stick.*]

MRS ROONEY: Now mind, here is the path . . . Up! . . . Well done! Now we are in safety and a straight run home.

MR ROONEY: [*Without halting, between gasps.*] A straight . . . run! . . . She calls that . . . a straight . . . run! . . .

MRS ROONEY: Hush! Do not speak as you go along, you know it is not good for your coronary. [*Dragging steps, etc.*] Just concentrate on putting one foot before the next or whatever the expression is. [*Dragging feet, etc.*] That is the way, now we are doing nicely. [*Dragging feet, etc. They suddenly halt, on* MRS ROONEY's *initiative.*] Heavens! I knew there was something! With all the excitement! I forgot!

MR ROONEY: [*Quietly.*] Good God!

MRS ROONEY: But you must know, Dan, of course, you were on
it. Whatever happened? Tell me!

MR ROONEY: I have never known anything to happen.

MRS ROONEY: But you must—

MR ROONEY: [*Violently.*] All this stopping and starting again is
devilish, devilish! I get a little way on me and begin to be
carried along when suddenly you stop dead! Two hundred
pounds of unhealthy fat! What possessed you to come out
at all? Let go of me!

MRS ROONEY: [*In great agitation.*] No, I must know, we won't
stir from here till you tell me. Fifteen minutes late! On a
thirty minute run! It's unheard of!

MR ROONEY: I know nothing. Let go of me before I shake you off.

MRS ROONEY: But you must know! You were on it! Was it at the
terminus? Did you leave on time? Or was it on the line?
[*Pause.*] Did something happen on the line? [*Pause.*] Dan!
[*Brokenly.*] Why won't you tell me!

[*Silence. They move off. Dragging feet, etc. They halt. Pause.*]

MR ROONEY: Poor Maddy! [*Pause. Children's cries.*] What was
that?

[*Pause for* MRS ROONEY *to ascertain.*]

MRS ROONEY: The Lynch twins jeering at us.

[*Cries.*]

MR ROONEY: Will they pelt us with mud today, do you suppose?
[*Cries.*]

MRS ROONEY: Let us turn and face them. [*Cries. They turn.
Silence.*] Threaten them with your stick. [*Silence.*] They have
run away.

[*Pause.*]

MR ROONEY: Did you ever wish to kill a child? [*Pause.*] Nip
some young doom in the bud. [*Pause.*] Many a time at
night, in winter, on the black road home, I nearly attacked
the boy. [*Pause.*] Poor Jerry! [*Pause.*] What restrained me
then? [*Pause.*] Not fear of man. [*Pause.*] Shall we go on
backwards now a little?

MRS ROONEY: Backwards?

23

MR ROONEY: Yes. Or you forwards and I backwards. The perfect pair. Like Dante's damned, with their faces arsy-versy. Our tears will water our bottoms.

MRS ROONEY: What is the matter, Dan? Are you not well?

MR ROONEY: Well! Did you ever know me to be well? The day you met me I should have been in bed. The day you proposed to me the doctors gave me up. You knew that, did you not? The night you married me they came for me with an ambulance. You have not forgotten that, I suppose? [*Pause.*] No, I cannot be said to be well. But I am no worse. Indeed I am better than I was. The loss of my sight was a great fillip. If I could go deaf and dumb I think I might pant on to be a hundred. Or have I done so? [*Pause.*] Was I a hundred today? [*Pause.*] Am I a hundred, Maddy? [*Silence.*]

MRS ROONEY: All is still. No living soul in sight. There is no one to ask. The world is feeding. The wind—[*Brief wind.*]—scarcely stirs the leaves and the birds—[*Brief chirp.*]—are tired singing. The cows—[*Brief moo.*]—and sheep—[*Brief baa.*]—ruminate in silence. The dogs—[*Brief bark.*]—are hushed and the hens—[*Brief cackle.*]—sprawl torpid in the dust. We are alone. There is no one to ask. [*Silence.*]

MR ROONEY: [*Clearing his throat, narrative tone.*] We drew out on the tick of time, I can vouch for that. I was—

MRS ROONEY: How can you vouch for it?

MR ROONEY: [*Normal tone, angrily.*] I can vouch for it, I tell you! Do you want my relation or don't you? [*Pause. Narrative tone.*] On the tick of time. I had the compartment to myself, as usual. At least I hope so, for I made no attempt to restrain myself. My mind— [*Normal tone.*] But why do we not sit down somewhere? Are we afraid we should never rise again?

MRS ROONEY: Sit down on what?

MR ROONEY: On a bench, for example.

MRS ROONEY: There is no bench.

MR ROONEY: Then on a bank, let us sink down upon a bank.

MRS ROONEY: There is no bank.

MR ROONEY: Then we cannot. [*Pause.*] I dream of other roads, in other lands. Of another home, another—[*He hesitates.*]—another home. [*Pause.*] What was I trying to say?

MRS ROONEY: Something about your mind.

MR ROONEY: [*Startled.*] My mind? Are you sure? [*Pause. Incredulous.*] My mind? . . . [*Pause.*] Ah yes. [*Narrative tone.*] Alone in the compartment my mind began to work, as so often after office hours, on the way home, in the train, to the lilt of the bogeys. Your season-ticket, I said, costs you twelve pounds a year and you earn, on an average, seven and six a day, that is to say barely enough to keep you alive and twitching with the help of food, drink, tobacco and periodicals until you finally reach home and fall into bed. Add to this— or subtract from it—rent, stationery, various subscriptions, tramfares to and fro, light and heat, permits and licences, hairtrims and shaves, tips to escorts, upkeep of premises and appearances, and a thousand unspecificable sundries, and it is clear that by lying at home in bed, day and night, winter and summer, with a change of pyjamas once a fortnight, you would add very considerably to your income. Business, I said— [*A cry. Pause. Again. Normal tone.*] Did I hear a cry?

MRS ROONEY: Mrs Tully I fancy. Her poor husband is in constant pain and beats her unmercifully.
[*Silence.*]

MR ROONEY: That was a short knock. [*Pause.*] What was I trying to get at?

MRS ROONEY: Business.

MR ROONEY: Ah yes, business. [*Narrative tone.*] Business, old man, I said, retire from business, it has retired from you. [*Normal tone.*] One has these moments of lucidity.

MRS ROONEY: I feel very cold and weak.

MR ROONEY: [*Narrative tone.*] On the other hand, I said, there are the horrors of home life, the dusting, sweeping, airing, scrubbing, waxing, waning, washing, mangling, drying,

25

mowing, clipping, raking, rolling, scuffling, shovelling, grinding, tearing, pounding, banging and slamming. And the brats, the happy little healthy little howling neighbours' brats. Of all this and much more the week-end, the Saturday intermission and then the day of rest, have given you some idea. But what must it be like on a working-day? A Wednesday? A Friday? What must it be like on a Friday! And I fell to thinking of my silent, backstreet, basement office, with its obliterated plate, rest-couch and velvet hangings, and what it means to be buried there alive, if only from ten to five, with convenient to the one hand a bottle of light pale ale and to the other a long ice-cold fillet of hake. Nothing, I said, not even fully certified death, can ever take the place of that. It was then I noticed that we were at a standstill. [*Pause. Normal tone. Irritably.*] Why are you hanging out of me like that? Have you swooned away?

MRS ROONEY: I feel very cold and faint. The wind—[*Whistling wind.*]—is whistling through my summer frock as if I had nothing on over my bloomers. I have had no solid food since my elevenses.

MR ROONEY: You have ceased to care. I speak—and you listen to the wind.

MRS ROONEY: No, no, I am agog, tell me all, then we shall press on and never pause, never pause, till we come safe to haven. [*Pause.*]

MR ROONEY: Never pause . . . safe to haven . . . Do you know, Maddy, sometimes one would think you were struggling with a dead language.

MRS ROONEY: Yes indeed, Dan, I know full well what you mean, I often have that feeling, it is unspeakably excruciating.

MR ROONEY: I confess I have it sometimes myself, when I happen to overhear what I am saying.

MRS ROONEY: Well, you know, it will be dead in time, just like our own poor dear Gaelic, there is that to be said. [*Urgent baa.*]

MR ROONEY: [*Startled.*] Good God!

MRS ROONEY: Oh the pretty little woolly lamb, crying to suck its mother! Theirs has not changed, since Arcady.
[*Pause.*]

MR ROONEY: Where was I in my composition?

MRS ROONEY: At a standstill.

MR ROONEY: Ah yes. [*Clears his throat. Narrative tone.*] I concluded naturally that we had entered a station and would soon be on our way again, and I sat on, without misgiving. Not a sound. Things are very dull today, I said, nobody getting down, nobody getting on. Then as time flew by and nothing happened I realized my error. We had not entered a station.

MRS ROONEY: Did you not spring up and poke your head out of the window?

MR ROONEY: What good would that have done me?

MRS ROONEY: Why to call out to be told what was amiss.

MR ROONEY: I did not care what was amiss. No, I just sat on, saying, If this train were never to move again I should not greatly mind. Then gradually a—how shall I say—a growing desire to—er—you know—welled up within me. Nervous probably. In fact now I am sure. You know, the feeling of being confined.

MRS ROONEY: Yes yes, I have been through that.

MR ROONEY: If we sit here much longer, I said, I really do not know what I shall do. I got up and paced to and fro between the seats, like a caged beast.

MRS ROONEY: That is a help sometimes.

MR ROONEY: After what seemed an eternity we simply moved off. And the next thing was Barrell bawling the abhorred name. I got down and Jerry led me to the men's, or Fir as they call it now, from Vir Viris I suppose, the V becoming F, in accordance with Grimm's Law. [*Pause.*] The rest you know. [*Pause.*] You say nothing? [*Pause.*] Say something. Maddy. Say you believe me.

MRS ROONEY: I remember once attending a lecture by one of these new mind doctors. I forget what you call them. He spoke—

MR ROONEY: A lunatic specialist?

MRS ROONEY: No no, just the troubled mind. I was hoping he might shed a little light on my lifelong preoccupation with horses' buttocks.

MR ROONEY: A neurologist.

MRS ROONEY: No no, just mental distress, the name will come back to me in the night. I remember his telling us the story of a little girl, very strange and unhappy in her ways, and how he treated her unsuccessfully over a period of years and was finally obliged to give up the case. He could find nothing wrong with her, he said. The only thing wrong with her as far as he could see was that she was dying. And she did in fact die, shortly after he had washed his hands of her.

MR ROONEY: Well? What is there so wonderful about that?

MRS ROONEY: No, it was just something he said, and the way he said it, that have haunted me ever since.

MR ROONEY: You lie awake at night, tossing to and fro and brooding on it.

MRS ROONEY: On it and other . . . wretchedness. [*Pause.*] When he had done with the little girl he stood there motionless for some time, quite two minutes I should say, looking down at his table. Then he suddenly raised his head and exclaimed, as if he had had a revelation, The trouble with her was she had never really been born! [*Pause.*] He spoke throughout without notes. [*Pause.*] I left before the end.

MR ROONEY: Nothing about your buttocks? [MRS ROONEY *weeps. In affectionate remonstrance.*] Maddy!

MRS ROONEY: There is nothing to be done for those people!

MR ROONEY: For which is there? [*Pause.*] That does not sound right somehow. [*Pause.*] What way am I facing?

MRS ROONEY: What?

MR ROONEY: I have forgotten what way I am facing.

MRS ROONEY: You have turned aside and are bowed down over the ditch.

MR ROONEY: There is a dead dog down there.

MRS ROONEY: No no, just the rotting leaves.

MR ROONEY: In June? Rotting leaves in June?

MRS ROONEY: Yes, dear, from last year, and from the year before last, and from the year before that again. [*Silence. Rainy wind. They move on. Dragging steps, etc.*] There is that lovely laburnum again. Poor thing, it is losing all its tassels. [*Dragging steps, etc.*] There are the first drops. [*Rain. Dragging steps, etc.*] Golden drizzle. [*Dragging steps, etc.*] Do not mind me, dear, I am just talking to myself. [*Rain heavier. Dragging steps, etc.*] Can hinnies procreate, I wonder? [*They halt.*]

MR ROONEY: Say that again.

MRS ROONEY: Come on, dear, don't mind me, we are getting drenched.

MR ROONEY: [*Forcibly.*] Can what what?

MRS ROONEY: Hinnies procreate. [*Silence.*] You know, hinnies, or jinnies, aren't they barren, or sterile, or whatever it is? [*Pause.*] It wasn't an ass's colt at all, you know, I asked the Regius Professor.

[*Pause.*]

MR ROONEY: He should know.

MRS ROONEY: Yes, it was a hinny, he rode into Jerusalem or wherever it was on a hinny. [*Pause.*] That must mean something. [*Pause.*] It's like the sparrows, than many of which we are of more value, they weren't sparrows at all.

MR ROONEY: Than many of which! . . . You exaggerate, Maddy.

MRS ROONEY: [*With emotion.*] They weren't sparrows at all!

MR ROONEY: Does that put our price up?

[*Silence. They move on. Wind and rain. Dragging feet, etc. They halt.*]

MRS ROONEY: Do you want some dung? [*Silence. They move on. Wind and rain, etc. They halt.*] Why do you stop? Do you want to say something?

MR ROONEY: No.

MRS ROONEY: Then why do you stop?

MR ROONEY: It is easier.

MRS ROONEY: Are you very wet?

MR ROONEY: To the buff.

MRS ROONEY: The buff?

MR ROONEY: The buff. From buffalo.

MRS ROONEY: We shall hang up all our things in the hot-cupboard and get into our dressing-gowns. [*Pause.*] Put your arm round me. [*Pause.*] Be nice to me! [*Pause. Gratefully.*] Ah, Dan! [*They move on. Wind and rain. Dragging feet, etc. Faintly same music as before. They halt. Music clearer. Silence but for music playing. Music dies.*] All day the same old record. All alone in that great empty house. She must be a very old woman now.

MR ROONEY: [*Indistinctly.*] Death and the Maiden.
    [*Silence.*]

MRS ROONEY: You are crying. [*Pause.*] Are you crying?

MR ROONEY: [*Violently.*] Yes! [*They move on. Wind and rain. Dragging feet, etc. They halt. They move on. Wind and rain. Dragging feet, etc. They halt.*] Who is the preacher tomorrow? The incumbent?

MRS ROONEY: No.

MR ROONEY: Thank God for that. Who?

MRS ROONEY: Hardy.

MR ROONEY: "How to be Happy though Married"?

MRS ROONEY: No no, he died, you remember. No connexion.

MR ROONEY: Has he announced his text?

MRS ROONEY: "The Lord upholdeth all that fall and raiseth up all those that be bowed down." [*Silence. They join in wild laughter. They move on. Wind and rain. Dragging feet, etc.*] Hold me tighter, Dan! [*Pause.*] Oh yes!
    [*They halt.*]

MR ROONEY: I hear something behind us.
    [*Pause.*]

MRS ROONEY: It looks like Jerry. [*Pause.*] It is Jerry.

[*Sound of* JERRY'*s running steps approaching. He halts beside them, panting.*]

JERRY: [*Panting.*] You dropped—

MRS ROONEY: Take your time, my little man, you will burst a blood-vessel.

JERRY: [*Panting.*] You dropped something, Sir. Mr Barrell told me to run after you.

MRS ROONEY: Show. [*She takes the object.*] What is it? [*She examines it.*] What is this thing, Dan?

MR ROONEY: Perhaps it is not mine at all.

JERRY: Mr Barrell said it was, Sir.

MRS ROONEY: It looks like a kind of ball. And yet it is not a ball.

MR ROONEY: Give it to me.

MRS ROONEY: [*Giving it.*] What *is* it, Dan?

MR ROONEY: It is a thing I carry about with me.

MRS ROONEY: Yes, but what—

MR ROONEY: [*Violently.*] It is a thing I carry about with me!
[*Silence.* MRS ROONEY *looks for a penny.*]

MRS ROONEY: I have no small money. Have you?

MR ROONEY: I have none of any kind.

MRS ROONEY: We are out of change, Jerry. Remind Mr Rooney on Monday and he will give you a penny for your pains.

JERRY: Yes, Ma'am.

MR ROONEY: If I am alive.

JERRY: Yessir.
[JERRY *starts running back towards the station.*]

MRS ROONEY: Jerry! [JERRY *halts.*] Did you hear what the hitch was? [*Pause.*] Did you hear what kept the train so late?

MR ROONEY: How would he have heard? Come on.

MRS ROONEY: What was it, Jerry?

JERRY: It was a—

MR ROONEY: Leave the boy alone, he knows nothing! Come on!

MRS ROONEY: What was it, Jerry?

JERRY: It was a little child, Ma'am.
[MR ROONEY *groans.*]

MRS ROONEY: What do you mean, it was a little child?

31

JERRY: It was a little child fell out of the carriage, Ma'am. [*Pause.*] On to the line, Ma'am. [*Pause.*] Under the wheels, Ma'am.

[*Silence. JERRY runs off. His steps die away. Tempest of wind and rain. It abates. They move on. Dragging steps, etc. They halt. Tempest of wind and rain.*]

END

Embers

A piece for radio

Written in English 1957–8 and completed February 1959. First broadcast on the BBC Third Programme on 24 June 1959. First published in *Evergreen Review* (November/December 1959).

HENRY
ADA
ADDIE
MUSIC MASTER / RIDING MASTER
PIANIST

Sea scarcely audible.
HENRY's *boots on shingle. He halts.*
Sea a little louder.

HENRY: On. [*Sea. Voice louder.*] On! [*He moves on. Boots on shingle. As he goes.*] Stop. [*Boots on shingle. As he goes, louder.*] Stop! [*He halts. Sea a little louder.*] Down. [*Sea. Voice louder.*] Down! [*Slither of shingle as he sits. Sea, still faint, audible throughout what follows whenever pause indicated.*] Who is beside me now? [*Pause.*] An old man, blind and foolish. [*Pause.*] My father, back from the dead, to be with me. [*Pause.*] As if he hadn't died. [*Pause.*] No, simply back from the dead, to be with me, in this strange place. [*Pause.*] Can he hear me? [*Pause.*] Yes, he must hear me. [*Pause.*] To answer me? [*Pause.*] No, he doesn't answer me. [*Pause.*] Just be with me. [*Pause.*] That sound you hear is the sea. [*Pause. Louder.*] I say that sound you hear is the sea, we are sitting on the strand. [*Pause.*] I mention it because the sound is so strange, so unlike the sound of the sea, that if you didn't see what it was you wouldn't know what it was. [*Pause.*] Hooves! [*Pause. Louder.*] Hooves! [*Sound of hooves walking on hard road. They die rapidly away. Pause.*] Again! [*Hooves as before. Pause. Excitedly.*] Train it to mark time! Shoe it with steel and tie it up in the yard, have it stamp all day! [*Pause.*] A ten-ton mammoth back from the dead, shoe it with steel and have it tramp the world down! [*Pause.*] Listen to it! [*Pause.*] Listen to the light now, you always loved light, not long past noon and all the shore in shadow and the sea out as far as the island. [*Pause.*] You would never live this side of the bay, you wanted the sun on the water for that evening

35

bathe you took once too often. But when I got your money I moved across, as perhaps you may know. [*Pause.*] We never found your body, you know, that held up probate an unconscionable time, they said there was nothing to prove you hadn't run away from us all and alive and well under a false name in the Argentine for example, that grieved mother greatly. [*Pause.*] I'm like you in that, can't stay away from it, but I never go in, no, I think the last time I went in was with you. [*Pause.*] Just be near it. [*Pause.*] Today it's calm, but I often hear it above in the house and walking the roads and start talking, oh just loud enough to drown it, nobody notices. [*Pause.*] But I'd be talking now no matter where I was, I once went to Switzerland to get away from the cursed thing and never stopped all the time I was there. [*Pause.*] I usen't to need anyone, just to myself, stories, there was a great one about an old fellow called Bolton, I never finished it, I never finished any of them, I never finished anything, everything always went on for ever. [*Pause.*] Bolton. [*Pause. Louder.*] Bolton! [*Pause.*] There before the fire. [*Pause.*] Before the fire with all the shutters . . . no, hangings, hangings, all the hangings drawn and the light, no light, only the light of the fire, sitting there in the . . . no, standing, standing there on the hearthrug in the dark before the fire with his arms on the chimney-piece and his head on his arms, standing there waiting in the dark before the fire in his old red dressing-gown and no sound in the house of any kind, only the sound of the fire. [*Pause.*] Standing there in his old red dressing-gown might go on fire any minute like when he was a child, no, that was his pyjamas, standing there waiting in the dark, no light, only the light of the fire, and no sound of any kind, only the fire, an old man in great trouble. [*Pause.*] Ring then at the door and over he goes to the window and looks out between the hangings, fine old chap, very big and strong, bright winter's night, snow everywhere, bitter cold, white world, cedar boughs bending under load and then as the arm goes up to ring again recognizes . . .

Holloway . . . [*Long pause.*] . . . yes, Holloway, recognizes Holloway, goes down and opens. [*Pause.*] Outside all still, not a sound, dog's chain maybe or a bough groaning if you stood there listening long enough, white world, Holloway with his little black bag, not a sound, bitter cold, full moon small and white, crooked trail of Holloway's galoshes, Vega in the Lyre very green. [*Pause.*] Vega in the Lyre very green. [*Pause.*] Following conversation then on the step, no, in the room, back in the room, following conversation then back in the room, Holloway: 'My dear Bolton, it is now past midnight, if you would be good enough—', gets no further, Bolton: 'Please! PLEASE!' Dead silence then, not a sound, only the fire, all coal, burning down now, Holloway on the hearthrug trying to toast his arse, Bolton, where's Bolton, no light, only the fire, Bolton at the window his back to the hangings, holding them a little apart with his hand looking out, white world, even the spire, white to the vane, most unusual, silence in the house, not a sound, only the fire, no flames now, embers. [*Pause.*] Embers. [*Pause.*] Shifting, lapsing, furtive like, dreadful sound, Holloway on the rug, fine old chap, six foot, burly, legs apart, hands behind his back holding up the tails of his old macfarlane, Bolton at the window, grand old figure in his old red dressing-gown, back against the hangings, hand stretched out widening the chink, looking out, white world great trouble, not a sound, only the embers, sound of dying, dying glow, Holloway, Bolton, Bolton, Holloway, old men, great trouble, white world, not a sound. [*Pause.*] Listen to it! [*Pause.*] Close your eyes and listen to it, what would you think it was? [*Pause. Vehement.*] A drip! A drip! [*Sound of drip, rapidly amplified, suddenly cut off.*] Again! [*Drip again. Amplification begins.*] No! [*Drip cut off. Pause.*] Father! [*Pause. Agitated.*] Stories, stories, years and years of stories, till the need came on me, for someone, to be with me, anyone, a stranger, to talk to, imagine he hears me, years of that, and then, now, for someone who . . . knew me, in the old days, anyone, to be

with me, imagine he hears me, what I am, now. [*Pause.*] No
good either. [*Pause.*] Not there either. [*Pause.*] Try again.
[*Pause.*] White world, not a sound. [*Pause.*] Holloway.
[*Pause.*] Holloway says he'll go, damned if he'll sit up all
night before a black grate, doesn't understand, call a man
out, an old friend, in the cold and dark, an old friend, urgent
need, bring the bag, then not a word, no explanation, no
heat, no light, Bolton: 'Please! PLEASE!' Holloway, no
refreshment, no welcome, chilled to the medulla, catch his
death, can't understand, strange treatment, old friend, says
he'll go, doesn't move, not a sound, fire dying, white beam
from window, ghastly scene, wishes to God he hadn't come,
no good, fire out, bitter cold, great trouble, white world, not
a sound, no good. [*Pause.*] No good. [*Pause.*] Can't do it.
[*Pause.*] Listen to it! [*Pause.*] Father! [*Pause.*] You wouldn't
know me now, you'd be sorry you ever had me, but you were
that already, a washout, that's the last I heard from you, a
washout. [*Pause. Imitating father's voice.*] 'Are you coming
for a dip?' 'No.' 'Come on, come on.' 'No.' Glare, stump to
door, turn, glare. 'A washout, that's all you are, a washout!'
[*Violent slam of door. Pause.*] Again! [*Slam. Pause.*] Slam life
shut like that! [*Pause.*] Washout. [*Pause.*] Wish to Christ she
had. [*Pause.*] Never met Ada, did you, or did you, I can't
remember, no matter, no one'd know her now. [*Pause.*]
What turned her against me do you think, the child I
suppose, horrid little creature, wish to God we'd never had
her, I used to walk with her in the fields, Jesus that was
awful, she wouldn't let go my hand and I mad to talk. 'Run
along now, Addie, and look at the lambs.' [*Imitating* ADDIE*'s
voice.*] 'No papa.' 'Go on now, go on.' [*Plaintive.*] 'No papa.'
[*Violent.*] 'Go on with you when you're told and look at the
lambs!' [ADDIE*'s loud wail. Pause.*] Ada too, conversation
with her, that was something, that's what hell will be like,
small chat to the babbling of Lethe about the good old days
when we wished we were dead. [*Pause.*] Price of margarine
fifty years ago. [*Pause.*] And now. [*Pause. With solemn indig-*

nation.] Price of blueband now! [*Pause.*] Father! [*Pause.*]
Tired of talking to you. [*Pause.*] That was always the way,
walk all over the mountains with you talking and talking and
then suddenly mum and home in misery and not a word to
a soul for weeks, sulky little bastard, better off dead, better
off dead. [*Long pause.*] Ada. [*Pause. Louder.*] Ada!

ADA: [*Low remote voice throughout.*] Yes.

HENRY: Have you been there long?

ADA: Some little time. [*Pause.*] Why do you stop, don't mind me.
[*Pause.*] Do you want me to go away? [*Pause.*] Where is
Addie?
[*Pause.*]

HENRY: With her music master. [*Pause.*] Are you going to
answer me today?

ADA: You shouldn't be sitting on the cold stones, they're bad for
your growths. Raise yourself up till I slip my shawl under
you. [*Pause.*] Is that better?

HENRY: No comparison, no comparison. [*Pause.*] Are you going
to sit down beside me?

ADA: Yes. [*No sound as she sits.*] Like that? [*Pause.*] Or do you
prefer like that? [*Pause.*] You don't care. [*Pause.*] Chilly
enough I imagine, I hope you put on your jaegers. [*Pause.*]
Did you put on your jaegers, Henry?

HENRY: What happened was this, I put them on and then I took
them off again and then I put them on again and then I took
them off again and then I took them on again and then I—

ADA: Have you them on now?

HENRY: I don't know. [*Pause.*] Hooves! [*Pause. Louder.*] Hooves!
[*Sound of hooves walking on hard road. They die rapidly
away.*] Again!
[*Hooves as before. Pause.*]

ADA: Did you hear them?

HENRY: Not well.

ADA: Galloping?

HENRY: No. [*Pause.*] Could a horse mark time?
[*Pause.*]

ADA: I'm not sure that I know what you mean.

HENRY: [*Irritably.*] Could a horse be trained to stand still and mark time with its four legs?

ADA: Oh. [*Pause.*] The ones I used to fancy all did. [*She laughs. Pause.*] Laugh, Henry, it's not every day I crack a joke. [*Pause.*] Laugh, Henry do that for me.

HENRY: You wish *me* to laugh?

ADA: You laughed so charmingly once, I think that's what first attracted me to you. That and your smile. [*Pause.*] Come on, it will be like old times.

[*Pause. He tries to laugh, fails.*]

HENRY: Perhaps I should begin with the smile. [*Pause for smile.*] Did that attract you? [*Pause.*] Now I'll try again. [*Long horrible laugh.*] Any of the old charm there?

ADA: Oh Henry!

[*Pause.*]

HENRY: Listen to it! [*Pause.*] Lips and claws! [*Pause.*] Get away from it! Where it couldn't get at me! The Pampas! What?

ADA: Calm yourself.

HENRY: And I live on the brink of it! Why? Professional obligations? [*Brief laugh.*] Reasons of health? [*Brief laugh.*] Family ties? [*Brief laugh.*] A woman? [*Laugh in which she joins.*] Some old grave I cannot tear myself away from? [*Pause.*] Listen to it! What is it like?

ADA: It is like an old sound I used to hear. [*Pause.*] It is like another time, in the same place. [*Pause.*] It was rough, the spray came flying over us. [*Pause.*] Strange it should have been rough then. [*Pause.*] And calm now.

[*Pause.*]

HENRY: Let us get up and go.

ADA: Go? Where? And Addie? She would be very distressed if she came and found you had gone without her. [*Pause.*] What do you suppose is keeping her?

[*Smart blow of cylindrical ruler on piano case. Unsteadily, ascending and descending,* ADDIE *plays scale of A Flat Major, hands first together, then reversed. Pause.*]

40

MUSIC MASTER: [*Italian accent.*] Santa Cecilia!
  [*Pause.*]
ADDIE: Will I play my piece now please?
  [*Pause.* MUSIC MASTER *beats two bars of waltz time with ruler on piano case.* ADDIE *plays opening bars of Chopin's 5th Waltz in A Flat Major,* MUSIC MASTER *beating time lightly with ruler as she plays. In first chord of bass, bar 5, she plays E instead of F. Resounding blow of ruler on piano case.* ADDIE *stops playing.*]
MUSIC MASTER: [*Violently.*] Fa!
ADDIE: [*Tearfully.*] What?
MUSIC MASTER: [*Violently.*] Eff! Eff!
ADDIE: [*Tearfully.*] Where?
MUSIC MASTER: [*Violently.*] Qua! [*He thumps note.*] Fa!
  [*Pause.* ADDIE *begins again,* MUSIC MASTER *beating time lightly with ruler. When she comes to bar 5 she makes same mistake. Tremendous blow of ruler on piano case.* ADDIE *stops playing, begins to wail.*]
MUSIC MASTER: [*Frenziedly.*] Eff! Eff! [*He hammers note.*] Eff!
  [*He hammers note.*] Eff!
  [*Hammered note, 'Eff!' and* ADDIE's *wail amplified to paroxysm, then suddenly cut off. Pause.*]
ADA: You are silent today.
HENRY: It was not enough to drag her into the world, now she must play the piano.
ADA: She must learn. She shall learn. That—and riding.
  [*Hooves walking.*]
RIDING MASTER: Now Miss! Elbows in Miss! Hands down Miss! [*Hooves trotting.*] Now Miss! Back straight Miss! Knees in Miss! [*Hooves cantering.*] Now Miss! Tummy in Miss! Chin up Miss! [*Hooves galloping.*] Now Miss! Eyes front Miss! [ADDIE *begins to wail.*] Now Miss! Now Miss!
  [*Galloping hooves, 'Now Miss!' and* ADDIE's *wail amplified to paroxysm, then suddenly cut off. Pause.*]
ADA: What are you thinking of? [*Pause.*] I was never taught, until it was too late. All my life I regretted it.

HENRY: What was your strong point, I forget.

ADA: Oh . . . geometry I suppose, plane and solid. [*Pause.*] First plane, then solid. [*Shingle as he gets up.*] Why do you get up?

HENRY: I thought I might try and get as far as the water's edge. [*Pause. With a sigh.*] And back. [*Pause.*] Stretch my old bones.

[*Pause.*]

ADA: Well, why don't you? [*Pause.*] Don't stand there thinking about it. [*Pause.*] Don't stand there staring. [*Pause. He goes towards sea. Boots on shingle, say ten steps. He halts at water's edge. Pause. Sea a little louder. Distant.*] Don't wet your good boots.

[*Pause.*]

HENRY: Don't, don't . . .

[*Sea suddenly rough.*]

ADA: [*Twenty years earlier, imploring.*] Don't! Don't!

HENRY: [*Ditto, urgent.*] Darling!

ADA: [*Ditto, more feebly.*] Don't!

HENRY: [*Ditto, exultantly.*] Darling!

[*Rough sea. ADA cries out. Cry and sea amplified, cut off. End of evocation. Pause. Sea calm. He goes back up deeply shelving beach. Boots laborious on shingle. He halts. Pause. He moves on. He halts. Pause. Sea calm and faint.*]

ADA: Don't stand there gaping. Sit down. [*Pause. Shingle as he sits.*] On the shawl. [*Pause.*] Are you afraid we might touch? [*Pause.*] Henry.

HENRY: Yes.

ADA: You should see a doctor about your talking, it's worse, what must it be like for Addie? [*Pause.*] Do you know what she said to me once, when she was still quite small, she said, Mummy, why does Daddy keep on talking all the time? She heard you in the lavatory. I didn't know what to answer.

HENRY: Daddy! Addie! [*Pause.*] I told you to tell her I was praying. [*Pause.*] Roaring prayers at God and his saints.

ADA: It's very bad for the child. [*Pause.*] It's silly to say it keeps you from hearing it, it doesn't keep you from hearing it and

42

even if it does you shouldn't be hearing it, there must be something wrong with your brain.

[*Pause.*]

HENRY: That! I shouldn't be hearing that!

ADA: I don't think you are hearing it. And if you are what's wrong with it, it's a lovely peaceful gentle soothing sound, why do you hate it? [*Pause.*] And if you hate it why don't you keep away from it? Why are you always coming down here? [*Pause.*] There's something wrong with your brain, you ought to see Holloway, he's alive still, isn't he?

[*Pause.*]

HENRY: [*Wildly.*] Thuds, I want thuds! Like this! [*He fumbles in the shingle, catches up two big stones and starts dashing them together.*] Stone! [*Clash.*] Stone! [*Clash. 'Stone!' and clash amplified, cut off. Pause. He throws one stone away. Sound of its fall.*] That's life! [*He throws the other stone away. Sound of its fall.*] Not this . . . [*Pause.*] . . . sucking!

ADA: And why life? [*Pause.*] Why life, Henry? [*Pause.*] Is there anyone about?

HENRY: Not a living soul.

ADA: I thought as much. [*Pause.*] When we longed to have it to ourselves there was always someone. Now that it does not matter the place is deserted.

HENRY: Yes, you were always very sensitive to being seen in gallant conversation. The least feather of smoke on the horizon and you adjusted your dress and became immersed in the *Manchester Guardian*. [*Pause.*] The hole is still there, after all these years. [*Pause. Louder.*] The hole is still there.

ADA: What hole? The earth is full of holes.

HENRY: Where we did it at last for the first time.

ADA: Ah yes, I think I remember. [*Pause.*] The place has not changed.

HENRY: Oh yes it has, *I* can see it. [*Confidentially.*] There is a levelling going on! [*Pause.*] What age is she now?

ADA: I have lost count of time.

HENRY: Twelve? Thirteen? [*Pause.*] Fourteen?

ADA: I really could not tell you, Henry.

HENRY: It took us a long time to have her. [*Pause.*] Years we kept hammering away at it. [*Pause.*] But we did it in the end. [*Pause. Sigh.*] We had her in the end. [*Pause.*] Listen to it! [*Pause.*] It's not so bad when you get out on it. [*Pause.*] Perhaps I should have gone into the merchant navy.

ADA: It's only on the surface, you know. Underneath all is as quiet as the grave. Not a sound. All day, all night, not a sound. [*Pause.*]

HENRY: Now I walk about with the gramophone. But I forgot it today.

ADA: There is no sense in that. [*Pause.*] There is no sense in trying to drown it. [*Pause.*] See Holloway. [*Pause.*]

HENRY: Let us go for a row.

ADA: A row? And Addie? She would be very distressed if she came and found you had gone for a row without her. [*Pause.*] Who were you with just now? [*Pause.*] Before you spoke to me.

HENRY: I was trying to be with my father.

ADA: Oh. [*Pause.*] No difficulty about that.

HENRY: I mean I was trying to get him to be with me. [*Pause.*] You seem a little cruder than usual today, Ada. [*Pause.*] I was asking him if he had ever met you, I couldn't remember.

ADA: Well?

HENRY: He doesn't answer any more.

ADA: I suppose you have worn him out. [*Pause.*] You wore him out living and now you are wearing him out dead. [*Pause.*] The time comes when one cannot speak to you any more. [*Pause.*] The time will come when no one will speak to you at all, not even complete strangers. [*Pause.*] You will be quite alone with your voice, there will be no other voice in the world but yours. [*Pause.*] Do you hear me? [*Pause.*]

HENRY: I can't remember if he met you.

44

ADA: You know he met me.

HENRY: No, Ada, I don't know, I'm sorry, I have forgotten almost everything connected with you.

ADA: You weren't there. Just your mother and sister. I had called to fetch you, as arranged. We were to go bathing together. [*Pause.*]

HENRY: [*Irritably.*] Drive on, drive on! Why do people always stop in the middle of what they are saying?

ADA: None of them knew where you were. Your bed had not been slept in. They were all shouting at one another. Your sister said she would throw herself off the cliff. Your father got up and went out, slamming the door. I left soon afterwards and passed him on the road. He did not see me. He was sitting on a rock looking out to sea. I never forgot his posture. And yet it was a common one. You used to have it sometimes. Perhaps just the stillness, as if he had been turned to stone. I could never make it out.
[*Pause.*]

HENRY: Keep on, keep on! [*Imploringly.*] Keep it going, Ada, every syllable is a second gained.

ADA: That's all, I'm afraid. [*Pause.*] Go on now with your father or your stories or whatever you were doing, don't mind me any more.

HENRY: I can't! [*Pause.*] I can't do it any more!

ADA: You were doing it a moment ago, before you spoke to me.

HENRY: [*Angrily.*] I can't do it any more now! [*Pause.*] Christ! [*Pause.*]

ADA: Yes, you know what I mean, there are attitudes remain in one's mind for reasons that are clear, the carriage of a head for example, bowed when one would have thought it should be lifted, and vice versa, or a hand suspended in mid-air, as if unowned. That kind of thing. But with your father sitting on the rock that day nothing of the kind, no detail you could put your finger on and say, How very peculiar! No, I could never make it out. Perhaps, as I said, just the great stillness of the whole body, as if all the breath

had left it. [*Pause.*] Is this rubbish a help to you, Henry?
[*Pause.*] I can try and go on a little if you wish. [*Pause.*] No?
[*Pause.*] Then I think I'll be getting back.

HENRY: Not yet! You needn't speak. Just listen. Not even. Be
with me. [*Pause.*] Ada! [*Pause. Louder.*] Ada! [*Pause.*]
Christ! [*Pause.*] Hooves! [*Pause. Louder.*] Hooves! [*Pause.*]
Christ! [*Long pause.*] Left soon afterwards, passed you on
the road, didn't see her, looking out to . . . [*Pause.*] Can't
have been looking out to *sea*. [*Pause.*] Unless you had gone
round the other side. [*Pause.*] Had you gone round the cliff
side? [*Pause.*] Father! [*Pause.*] Must have I suppose.
[*Pause.*] Stands watching you a moment then on down path
to tram, up on open top and sits down in front. [*Pause.*] Sits
down in front. [*Pause.*] Suddenly feels uneasy and gets
down again, conductor: 'Changed your mind, Miss?', goes
back up path, no sign of you. [*Pause.*] Very unhappy and
uneasy, hangs round a bit, not a soul about, cold wind
coming in off sea, goes back down path and takes tram
home. [*Pause.*] Takes tram home. [*Pause.*] Christ! [*Pause.*]
'My dear Bolton . . .' [*Pause.*] 'If it's an injection you want,
Bolton, let down your trousers and I'll give you one, I have
a panhysterectomy at nine,' meaning of course the anaes-
thetic. [*Pause.*] Fire out, bitter cold, white world, great
trouble, not a sound. [*Pause.*] Bolton starts playing with the
curtain, no, hanging, difficult to describe, draws it back no,
kind of gathers it towards him and the moon comes flooding in, then lets it fall back, heavy velvet affair, and pitch
black in the room, then towards him again, white, black,
white, black, Holloway: 'Stop that for the love of God,
Bolton, do you want to finish me?' [*Pause.*] Black, white,
black, white, maddening thing. [*Pause.*] Then he suddenly
strikes a match, Bolton does, lights a candle, catches it up
above his head, walks over and looks Holloway full in the
eye. [*Pause.*] Not a word, just the look, the old blue eye,
very glassy, lids worn thin, lashes gone, whole thing swim-
ming, and the candle shaking over his head. [*Pause.*] Tears?

46

[*Pause. Long laugh.*] Good God no! [*Pause.*] Not a word, just the look, the old blue eye, Holloway: 'If you want a shot say so and let me get to hell out of here.' [*Pause.*] 'We've had this before, Bolton, don't ask me to go through it again.' [*Pause.*] Bolton: 'Please!' [*Pause.*] 'Please!' [*Pause.*] 'Please, Holloway!' [*Pause.*] Candle shaking and guttering all over the place, lower now, old arm tired takes it in the other hand and holds it high again, that's it, that was always it, night, and the embers cold, and the glim shaking in your old fist, saying, Please! Please! [*Pause.*] Begging. [*Pause.*] Of the poor. [*Pause.*] Ada! [*Pause.*] Father! [*Pause.*] Christ! [*Pause.*] Holds it high again, naughty world, fixes Holloway, eyes drowned, won't ask again, just the look, Holloway covers his face, not a sound, white world, bitter cold, ghastly scene, old men, great trouble, no good. [*Pause.*] No good. [*Pause.*] Christ! [*Pause. Shingle as he gets up. He goes towards sea. Boots on shingle. He halts. Pause. Sea a little louder.*] On. [*Pause. He moves on. Boots on shingle. He halts at water's edge. Pause. Sea a little louder.*] Little book. [*Pause.*] This evening . . . [*Pause.*] Nothing this evening. [*Pause.*] Tomorrow . . . tomorrow . . . plumber at nine, then nothing. [*Pause. Puzzled.*] Plumber at nine? [*Pause.*] Ah yes, the waste. [*Pause.*] Words. [*Pause.*] Saturday . . . nothing. Sunday . . . Sunday . . . Nothing all day. [*Pause.*] Nothing, all day nothing. [*Pause.*] All day all night nothing. [*Pause.*] Not a sound.

Sea.

47

Rough for Radio I

Written in French in late 1961. First published in English as 'Sketch for Radio Play' in *Stereo Headphones*, no. 7 (Spring 1976).

HE
SHE
MUSIC
VOICE

HE: [*Gloomily.*] Madam.

SHE: Are you all right? [*Pause.*] You asked me to come.

HE: I ask no one to come here.

SHE: You suffered me to come.

HE: I meet my debts.
    [*Pause.*]

SHE: I have come to listen.

HE: When you please.
    [*Pause.*]

SHE: May I squat on this hassock? [*Pause.*] Thank you.
    [*Pause.*] May we have a little heat?

HE: No, Madam.
    [*Pause.*]

SHE: Is it true the music goes on all the time?

HE: Yes.

SHE: Without cease?

HE: Without cease?

SHE: It's unthinkable! [*Pause.*] And the words too? All the time
    too?

HE: All the time.

SHE: Without cease?

HE: Yes.

SHE: It's unimaginable. [*Pause.*] So you are here all the time?

HE: Without cease.
    [*Pause.*]

SHE: How troubled you look! [*Pause.*] May one see them?

HE: No, Madam.

SHE: I may not go and see them?

HE: No, Madam.
    [*Pause.*]

SHE: May we have a little light?

HE: No, Madam.
  [*Pause.*]

SHE: How cold you are! [*Pause.*] Are these the two knobs?

HE: Yes.

SHE: Just push? [*Pause.*] Is it live? [*Pause.*] I ask you is it live.

HE: No, you must twist. [*Pause.*] To the right.
  [*Click.*]

MUSIC: [*Faint.*] . . . .
  [*Silence.*]

SHE: [*Astonished.*] But there are more than one!

HE: Yes.

SHE: How many?
  [*Pause.*]

HE: To the right, Madam, to the right.
  [*Click.*]

VOICE: [*Faint.*] . . . .

SHE: [*With voice.*] Louder!

VOICE: [*No louder.*] . . . .
  [*Silence.*]

SHE: [*Astonished.*] But he is alone!

HE: Yes.

SHE: All alone?

HE: When one is alone one is all alone.
  [*Pause.*]

SHE: What is it like together?
  [*Pause.*]

HE: To the right, Madam.
  [*Click.*]

MUSIC: [*Faint, brief.*] . . . .

MUSIC: } [*Together.*] . . . .
VOICE:
  [*Silence.*]

SHE: They are not together?

HE: No.

SHE: They cannot see each other?

HE: No.

SHE: Hear each other?

HE: No.

SHE: It's inconceivable!
    [*Pause.*]

HE: To the right, Madam.
    [*Click.*]

VOICE: [*Faint.*] . . . .

SHE: [*With voice.*] Louder!

VOICE: [*No louder.*] . . . .
    [*Silence.*]

SHE: And—[*Faint stress.*]—*you* like that?

HE: It is a need.

SHE: A need? *That* a need?

HE: It has become a need. [*Pause.*] To the right, Madam.
    [*Click.*]

MUSIC: [*Faint.*] . . . .

SHE: [*With music.*] Louder!

MUSIC: [*No louder.*] . . . .
    [*Silence.*]

SHE: That too? [*Pause.*] That a need too?

HE: It has become a need, Madam.

SHE: Are they in the same . . . situation?
    [*Pause.*]

HE: I don't understand.

SHE: Are they . . . subject to the same . . . conditions?

HE: Yes, Madam.

SHE: For instance? [*Pause.*] For instance?

HE: One cannot describe them, Madam.
    [*Pause.*]

SHE: Well, I'm obliged to you.

HE: Allow me, this way.
    [*Pause.*]

SHE: [*A little off.*] Is that a Turkoman?

HE: [*Ditto.*] Allow me.

SHE: [*A little further off.*] How troubled you look! [*Pause.*]

53

Well, I'll leave you. [*Pause.*] To your needs.

HE: [*Ditto.*] Good-bye, Madam. [*Pause.*] To the right, Madam, that's the garbage—[*Faint stress.*]—the *house* garbage. [*Pause.*] Good-bye, Madam.

[*Long pause. Sound of curtains violently drawn, first one, then the other, clatter of the heavy rings along the rods. Pause. Faint ping—as sometimes happens—of telephone receiver raised from cradle. Faint sound of dialing. Pause.*] Hello . . . Miss . . . is the doctor . . . ah . . . yes . . . he to call me . . . Macgillycuddy . . . Mac-gilly-cuddy . . . right . . . he'll know . . . and Miss . . . Miss! . . . urgent . . . yes! . . . [*Shrill.*] . . . most urgent!

[*Pause. Receiver put down with same faint ping. Pause. Click.*]

MUSIC: [*Faint.*] . . . .

HE: [*With music.*] Good God!

MUSIC: [*Faint.*] . . . .

[*Silence. Pause. Click.*]

VOICE: [*Faint.*] . . . .

HE: [*With voice, shrill.*] Come on! Come on!

VOICE: [*Faint.*] . . . .

[*Silence.*]

HE: [*Low.*] What'll I do? [*Pause. Faint ping of receiver raised again. Faint dialling. Pause.*] Hello . . . Miss . . . Macgillycuddy . . . Mac-gilly-cuddy . . . right . . . I'm sorry but . . . ah . . . yes . . . of course . . . can't reach him . . . no idea . . . understand . . . right . . . immediately . . . the moment he gets back . . . what? . . . [*Shrill.*] . . . yes! . . . I told you so! . . . most urgent! . . . most urgent! . . . [*Pause. Low.*] Slut!

[*Sound of receiver put down violently. Pause. Click.*]

MUSIC: [*Faint. Brief.*] . . . .

[*Silence. Click.*]

VOICE: [*Faint. Brief.*] . . . .

HE: [*With voice, shrill.*] It's crazy! Like one!

MUSIC: ⎤
            ⎥ [*Together.*] . . . .
        ⎦

[*Telephone rings. Receiver raised immediately, not more than a second's ring.*]

HE: [*With music and voice.*] Yes . . . wait . . . [*Music and voice silent. Very agitated.*] Yes . . . yes . . . no matter . . . what the trouble is? . . . they're ending . . . ENDING . . . this morning . . . what? . . . no! . . . no question! . . . ENDING I tell you . . . nothing what? . . . to be done? . . . I know there's nothing to be done . . . what? . . . no! . . . it's me . . . ME . . . what? I tell you they're ending . . . ENDING . . . I can't stay like that after . . . who? . . . but she's left me . . . ah for God's sake . . . haven't they all left me? . . . did you not know that? . . . all left me . . . sure? . . . of course I'm sure . . . what? . . . in an hour? . . . not before? . . . wait . . . [*Low.*] . . . there's more . . . they're together . . . TOGETHER . . . yes . . . I don't know . . . like . . . [*Hesitation.*] . . . one . . . the breathing . . . I don't know . . . [*Vehement.*] . . . no! . . . never! . . . meet? . . . how could they meet? . . . what? . . . what are all alike? . . . last what? . . . gasps? . . . wait . . . don't go yet . . . wait! . . . [*Pause. Sound of receiver put down violently. Low.*] Swine!

[*Pause. Click.*]

MUSIC: [*Failing.*] . . . .

MUSIC: ⎤
⎥ [*Together, failing.*] . . . .
VOICE: ⎦

[*Telephone rings. Receiver immediately raised.*]

HE: [*With music and voice.*] Miss . . . what? . . . [*Music and voice silent.*] . . . a confinement? . . . [*Long pause.*] . . . two confinements? . . . [*Long pause.*] . . . one what? . . . what? . . . breech? . . . what? . . . [*Long pause.*] . . . tomorrow noon? . . .

[*Long pause. Faint ping as receiver put gently down. Long pause. Click.*]

MUSIC: [*Brief, failing.*] . . . .

MUSIC: ⎤ [*Together, ending, breaking off together, resuming together
⎥ more and more feebly.*] . . . .
VOICE: ⎦

[*Silence. Long pause.*]

HE: [*Whisper.*] Tomorrow . . . noon . . .

Rough for Radio II

Written in French in the early 1960s. First broadcast under the title 'Rough for Radio' on BBC Radio 3 on 13 April 1976. First published in English by Grove Press, New York, in 1976.

ANIMATOR
STENOGRAPHER
FOX
DICK (mute)

A: Ready, Miss?

S: And waiting, Sir.

A: Fresh pad, spare pencils?

S: The lot, Sir.

A: Good shape?

S: Tiptop, Sir.

A: And you, Dick, on your toes? [*Swish of bull's pizzle. Admiringly.*] Wow! Let's hear it land. [*Swish and formidable thud.*] Good. Off with his hood. [*Pause.*] Ravishing face, ravishing! Is it not, Miss?

S: Too true, Sir. We know it by heart and yet the pang is ever new.

A: The gag. [*Pause.*] The blind. [*Pause.*] The plugs. [*Pause.*] Good. [*He thumps on his desk with a cylindrical ruler.*] Fox, open your eyes, readjust them to the light of day and look about you. [*Pause.*] You see, the same old team. I hope—

S: [*Aflutter.*] Oh!

A: What is it, Miss? Vermin in the lingerie?

S: He smiled at me!

A: Good omen. [*Faint hope.*] Not the first time by any chance?

S: Heavens no, Sir, what an idea!

A: [*Disappointed.*] I might have known. [*Pause.*] And yet it still affects you?

S: Why yes, Sir, it is so sudden! So radiant! So fleeting!

A: You note it?

S: Oh no, Sir, the words alone. [*Pause.*] Should one note the play of feature too?

A: I don't know, Miss. Depending perhaps.

S: Me you know—

A: [*Trenchant.*] Leave it for the moment. [*Thump with ruler.*] Fox, I hope you have had a refreshing night and will be better inspired today than heretofore. Miss.

S: Sir.

A: Let us hear again the report on yesterday's results, it has somewhat slipped my memory.

S: [*Reading.*] 'We the undersigned, assembled under—'

A: Skip.

S: [*Reading.*] '. . . note yet again with pain that these dicta—'

A: Dicta! [*Pause.*] Read on.

S: '. . . with pain that these dicta, like all those communicated to date and by reason of the same deficiencies, are totally inacceptable. The second half in particular is of such—'

A: Skip.

S: '. . . outlook quite hopeless were it not for our conviction—'

A: Skip. [*Pause.*] Well?

S: That is all, Sir.

A: . . . same deficiencies . . . totally inacceptable . . . outlook quite hopeless . . . [*Disgusted.*] Well! [*Pause.*] Well!

S: That is all, Sir. Unless I am to read the exhortations.

A: Read them.

S: '. . . instantly renew our standing exhortations, namely:
   1. Kindly to refrain from recording mere animal cries, they serve only to indispose us.
   2. Kindly to provide a strictly literal transcript, the meanest syllable has, or may have, its importance.
   3. Kindly to ensure full neutralization of the subject when not in session, especially with regard to the gag, its permanence and good repair. Thus rigid enforcement of the tube-feed, be it per buccam or be it on the other hand per rectum, is *absolutely*'—one word underlined—'essential. The least word let fall in solitude and thereby in danger, as Mauthner has shown, of being no longer needed, *may be it*'—three words underlined.
   '4. Kindly—'

A: Enough! [*Sickened.*] Well! [*Pause.*] Well!

s: It is past two, Sir.

a: [*Roused from his prostration.*] It is what?

s: Past two, Sir.

a: [*Roughly.*] Then what are you waiting for? [*Pause. Gently.*] Forgive me, Miss, forgive me, my cup is full. [*Pause.*] Forgive me!

s: [*Coldly.*] Shall I open with yesterday's close?

a: If you would be so good.

s: [*Reading.*] 'When I had done soaping the mole, thoroughly rinsing and drying before the embers, what next only out again in the blizzard and put him back in his chamber with his weight of grubs, at that instant his little heart was beating still I swear, ah my God my God.' [*She strikes with her pencil on her desk.*] 'My God.'
[*Pause.*]

a: Unbelievable! And there he jibbed, if I remember aright.

s: Yes, Sir, he would say no more.

a: Dick functioned?

s: Let me see . . . Yes, twice.
[*Pause.*]

a: Does not the glare incommode you, Miss, what if we should let down the blind?

s: Thank you, Sir, not on my account, it can never be too warm, never too bright, for me. But, with your permission, I shall shed my overall.

a: [*With alacrity.*] Please do, Miss, please do. [*Pause.*] Staggering! Staggering! Ah were I but . . . forty years younger!

s: [*Rereading.*] 'Ah my God my God.' [*Blow with pencil.*] 'My God.'

a: Crabbed youth! No pity! [*Thump with ruler.*] Do you mark me? On! [*Silence.*] Dick! [*Swish and thud of pizzle on flesh. Faint cry from* FOX.] Off record, Miss, remember?

s: Drat it! Where's that eraser?

a: Erase, Miss, erase, we're in trouble enough already. [*Ruler.*] On! [*Silence.*] Dick!

F: Ah yes, that for sure, live I did, no denying, all stones all sides—

A: One moment.

F: —walls no further—

A: [*Ruler.*] Silence! Dick! [*Silence. Musing.*] Live I did . . . [*Pause.*] Has he used that turn before, Miss?

S: To what turn do you allude, Sir?

A: Live I did.

S: Oh yes, Sir, it's a notion crops up now and then. Perhaps not in those precise terms, so far, that I could not say offhand. But allusions to a life, though not common, are not rare.

A: His own life?

S: Yes, Sir, a life all his own.

A: [*Disappointed.*] I might have known. [*Pause.*] What a memory—mine! [*Pause.*] Have you read the Purgatory, Miss, of the divine Florentine?

S: Alas no, Sir. I have merely flipped through the Inferno.

A: [*Incredulous.*] Not read the Purgatory?

S: Alas no, Sir.

A: There all sigh, I was, I was. It's like a knell. Strange, is it not?

S: In what sense, Sir?

A: Why, one would rather have expected, I shall be. No?

S: [*With tender condescension.*] The creatures! [*Pause.*] It is getting on for three, Sir.

A: [*Sigh.*] Good. Where were we?

S: '. . . walls no further—'

A: Before, that, Miss, the house is not on fire.

S: '. . . live I did, no denying, all stones all sides'—inaudible— 'walls—'

A: [*Ruler.*] On! [*Silence.*] Dick!

S: Sir.

A: [*Impatiently.*] What is it, Miss, can't you see that old time is aflying?

S: I was going to suggest a touch of kindness, Sir, perhaps just a hint of kindness.

A: So soon? And then? [*Firmly.*] No, Miss, I appreciate your sentiment. But I have my method. Shall I remind you of it?

62

[*Pause. Pleading.*] Don't say no! [*Pause.*] Oh you are an angel! You may sit, Dick. [*Pause.*] In a word, REDUCE the pressure instead of increasing it. [*Lyrical.*] Caress, fount of resipescence! [*Calmer.*] Dick, if you would. [*Swish and thud of pizzle on flesh. Faint cry from* FOX.] Careful, Miss.

S: Have no fear, Sir.

A: [*Ruler.*] . . . walls . . . walls what?

S: 'no further', Sir.

A: Right. [*Ruler.*] . . . walls no further . . . [*Ruler.*] On! [*Silence.*] Dick!

F: That for sure, no further, and there gaze, all the way up, all the way down, slow gaze, age upon age, up again, down again, little lichens of my own span, living dead in the stones, and there took to the tunnels. [*Silence. Ruler.*] Oceans too, that too, no denying, I drew near down the tunnels, blue above, blue ahead, that for sure, and there too, no further, ways end, all ends and farewell, farewell and fall, farewell seasons, till I fare again. [*Silence. Ruler.*] Farewell.
   [*Silence. Ruler. Pause.*]

A: Dick!

F: That for sure, no denying, no further, down in Spring, up in Fall, or inverse, such summers missed, such winters.
   [*Pause.*]

A: Nice! Nicely put! Such summers missed! So sibilant! Don't you agree, Miss?

F: ⎫
   ⎬ [*Together.*] Ah that for sure—
S: ⎭   Oh me you know—

A: Hsst!

F: — fatigue, what fatigue, my brother inside me, my old twin, ah to be he and he—but no, no no. [*Pause.*] No no. [*Silence. Ruler.*] Me get up, me go on, what a hope, it was he, for hunger. Have yourself opened, Maud would say, opened up, it's nothing, I'll give him suck if he's still alive, ah but no, no no. [*Pause.*] No no.
   [*Silence.*]

A: [*Discouraged.*] Ah dear.

s: He is weeping, Sir, shall I note it?

a: I really do not know what to advise, Miss.

s: Inasmuch as . . . how shall I say? . . . human trait . . . can one say in English?

a: I have never come across it, Miss, but no doubt.

f: Scrabble scrabble—

a: Silence! [*Pause.*] No holding him!

s: As such . . . I feel . . . perhaps . . . at a pinch . . .
      [*Pause.*]

a: Are you familiar with the works of Sterne, Miss?

s: Alas no, Sir.

a: I may be quite wrong, but I seem to remember, there somewhere, a tear an angel comes to catch as it falls. Yes, I seem to remember . . . admittedly he was grandchild to an archbishop. [*Half rueful, half complacent.*] Ah these old spectres from the days of book reviewing, they lie in wait for one at every turn. [*Pause. Suddenly decided.*] Note it, Miss, note it, and come what may. As well as for a sheep . . . [*Pause.*] Who is this woman . . . what's the name?

s: Maud. I don't know, Sir, no previous mention of her has been made.

a: [*Excited.*] Are you sure?

s: Positive, Sir. You see, my nanny was a Maud, so that the name would have struck me, had it been pronounced.
      [*Pause.*]

a: I may be quite wrong, but I somehow have the feeling this is the first time—oh I know it's a far call!—that he has actually . . . *named* anyone. No?

s: That may well be, Sir. To make sure I would have to check through from the beginning. That would take time.

a: Kith and kin?

s: Never a word, Sir. I have been struck by it. Mine play such a part, in my life!

a: And of a sudden, in the same sentence, a woman, with Christian name to boot, and a brother. I ask you!
      [*Pause.*]

64

s: That twin, Sir . . .

A: I know, not very convincing.

s: [*Scandalized.*] But it's quite simply impossible! Inside him! *Him!*

A: No no, such things happen, such things happen. Nature, you know . . . [*Faint laugh.*] Fortunately. A world without monsters, just imagine! [*Pause for imagining.*] No, that is not what troubles me. [*Warmly.*] Look you, Miss, what counts is not so much the *thing*, in itself, that would astonish me too. No, it's the word, the notion. The notion brother is not unknown to him! [*Pause.*] But what really matters is this woman—what name did you say?

s: Maud, Sir.

A: Maud!

s: And who is in milk, what is more, or about to be.

A: For mercy's sake! [*Pause.*] How does the passage go again?

s: [*Rereading.*] 'Me get up, me go on, what a hope, it was he, for hunger. Have yourself opened, Maud would say, opened up, it's nothing, I'll give him suck if he's still alive, ah but no, no no.' [*Pause.*] 'No no.'
   [*Pause.*]

A: And then the tear.

s: Exactly, Sir. What I call the human trait.
   [*Pause.*]

A: [*Low, with emotion.*] Miss.

s: Sir.

A: Can it be we near our goal. [*Pause.*] Oh how bewitching you look when you show your teeth! Ah were I but . . . thirty years younger.

s: It is well after three, Sir.

A: [*Sigh.*] Good. Where he left off. Once more.

s: 'Oh but no, no—'

A: *Ah* but no. No?

s: You are quite right, Sir. 'Ah but no, no—'

A: [*Severely.*] Have a care, Miss.

s: 'Ah but no, no no.' [*Pause.*] 'No, no.'

A: [*Ruler.*] On! [*Silence.*] Dick!

s: He has gone off, Sir.

A: Just a shade lighter, Dick. [*Mild thud of pizzle.*] Ah no, you exaggerate, better than that. [*Swish and violent thud. Faint cry from* FOX. *Ruler.*] Ah but no, no no. On!

F: [*Scream.*] Let me out! Peter out in the stones!

A: Ah dear! There he goes again. Peter out in the stones!

s: It's a mercy he's tied.

A: [*Gently.*] Be reasonable, Fox. Stop—you may sit, Dick—stop jibbing. It's hard on you, we know. It does not lie entirely with us, we know. You might prattle away to your latest breath and still the one . . . thing remain unsaid that can give you back your darling solitudes, we know. But this much is sure: the more you say the greater your chances. Is that not so, Miss?

s: It stands to reason, Sir.

A: [*As to a backward pupil.*] Don't ramble! Treat the subject, whatever it is! [*Snivel.*] More variety! [*Snivel.*] Those everlasting wilds may have their charm, but there is nothing there for us, that would astonish me. [*Snivel.*] Those micaceous schists, if you knew the effect [*Snivel.*] they can have on one, in the long run. [*Snivel.*] And your fauna! Those fodient rodents! [*Snivel.*] You wouldn't have a handkerchief, Miss, you could lend me?

s: Here you are, Sir.

A: Most kind. [*Blows nose abundantly.*] Much obliged.

s: Oh you may keep it, Sir.

A: No no, now I'll be all right. [*To* FOX.] Of course we do not know, any more than you, what exactly it is we are after, what sign or set of words. But since you have failed so far to let it escape you, it is not by harking on the same old themes that you are likely to succeed, that would astonish me.

s: He has gone off again, Sir.

A: [*Warming to his point.*] Someone, perhaps that is what is wanting, someone who once saw you . . . [*Abating.*] . . . go

66

by. I may be quite wrong, but try, at least, what do you stand to lose? [*Beside himself.*] Even though it is not true!

S: [*Shocked.*] Oh Sir!

A: A father, a mother, a friend, a . . . Beatrice—no, that is asking too much. Simply someone, anyone, who once saw you . . . go by. [*Pause.*] That woman . . . what's the name?

S: Maud, Sir.

A: That Maud, for example, perhaps you once brushed against each other. Think hard!

S: He has gone off, Sir.

A: Dick!—no, wait. Kiss him, Miss, perhaps that will stir some fibre.

S: Where, Sir?

A: In his heart, in his entrails—or some other part.

S: No, I mean kiss him where, Sir?

A: [*Angry.*] Why on his stinker of a mouth, what do you suppose? [STENOGRAPHER *kisses* FOX. *Howl from* FOX.] Till it bleeds! Kiss it white! [*Howl from* FOX.] Suck his gullet! [*Silence.*]

S: He has fainted away, Sir.

A: Ah . . . perhaps I went too far. [*Pause.*] Perhaps I slipped you too soon.

S: Oh no, Sir, you could not have waited a moment longer, time is up. [*Pause.*] The fault is mine, I did not go about it as I ought.

A: Come, come, Miss! To the marines! [*Pause.*] Up already! [*Pained.*] I chatter too much.

S: Come, come, Sir, don't say that, it is part of your rôle, as animator.
   [*Pause.*]

A: That tear, Miss, do you remember?

S: Oh yes, Sir, distinctly.

A: [*Faint hope.*] Not the first time by any chance?

S: Heavens no, Sir, what an idea!

A: [*Disappointed.*] I might have known.

S: Last winter, now I come to think of it, he shed several, do you not remember?

A: Last winter! But, my dear child, I don't remember yesterday, it is down the hatch with love's young dream. Last winter! [*Pause. Low, with emotion.*] Miss.

S: [*Low.*] Sir.

A: That . . . Maud.
    [*Pause.*]

S: [*Encouraging.*] Yes, Sir.

A: Well . . . you know . . . I may be wrong . . . I wouldn't like to . . . I hardly dare say it . . . but it seems to me that . . . here . . . possibly . . . we have something at last.

S: Would to God, Sir.

A: Particularly with that tear so hard behind. It is not the first, agreed. But in such a context!

S: And the milk, Sir, don't forget the milk.

A: The breast! One can almost see it!

S: Who got her in that condition, there's another question for us.

A: What condition, Miss, I fail to follow you.

S: Someone has fecundated her. [*Pause. Impatient.*] If she is in milk someone must have fecundated her.

A: To be sure!

S: Who?

A: [*Very excited.*] You mean . . .

S: I ask myself.
    [*Pause.*]

A: May we have that passage again, Miss?

S: 'Have yourself opened, Maud would say, opened—'

A: [*Delighted.*] That frequentative! [*Pause.*] Sorry, Miss.

S: 'Have yourself opened, Maud would say, opened—'

A: Don't skip, Miss, the text in its entirety if you please.

S: I skip nothing, Sir. [*Pause.*] What have I skipped, Sir?

A: [*Emphatically.*] '. . . between two kisses . . .' [*Sarcastic.*] That mere trifle! [*Angry.*] How can we ever hope to get anywhere if you suppress gems of that magnitude?

S: But, Sir, he never said anything of the kind.

A: [*Angry.*] '. . . Maud would say, *between two kisses*, etc.' Amend.

68

S: But, Sir, I—

A: What the devil are you deriding, Miss? My hearing? My memory? My good faith? [*Thunderous.*] Amend!

S: [*Feebly.*] As you will, Sir.

A: Let us hear how it runs now.

S: [*Tremulous.*] 'Have yourself opened, Maud would say, between two kisses, opened up, it's nothing, I'll give him suck if he's still alive, ah but no, no no.' [*Faint pencil.*] 'No no.'
[*Silence.*]

A: Don't cry, Miss, dry your pretty eyes and smile at me. Tomorrow, who knows, we may be free.

Words and Music

A piece for radio

Written in English and completed towards the end of 1961. First broadcast on the BBC Third Programme on 13 November 1962. First published in *Evergreen Review* (November/December 1962).

MUSIC
CROAK
WORDS

MUSIC: *Small orchestra softly tuning up.*

WORDS: Please! [*Tuning. Louder.*] Please! [*Tuning dies away.*] How much longer cooped up here in the dark? [*With loathing.*] With you! [*Pause.*] Theme. . . . [*Pause.*] Theme . . . sloth. [*Pause. Rattled off, low.*] Sloth is of all the passions the most powerful passion and indeed no passion is more powerful than the passion of sloth, this is the mode in which the mind is most affected and indeed—[*Burst of tuning. Loud, imploring.*] Please! [*Tuning dies away. As before.*] The mode in which the mind is most affected and indeed in no mode is the mind more affected than in this, by passion we are to understand a movement of the soul pursuing or fleeing real or imagined pleasure or pain pleasure or pain real or imagined pleasure or pain, of all these movements and who can number them of all these movements and they are legion sloth is the most urgent and indeed by no movement is the soul more urged than by this by this by this to and from by no movement the soul more urged than by this to and—[*Pause.*] From. [*Pause.*] Listen! [*Distant sound of rapidly shuffling carpet slippers.*] At last! [*Shuffling louder. Burst of tuning.*] Hsst! [*Tuning dies away. Shuffling louder. Silence.*]

CROAK: Joe.

WORDS: [*Humble.*] My Lord.

CROAK: Bob.

MUSIC: *Humble muted adsum.*

CROAK: My comforts! Be friends! [*Pause.*] Bob.

MUSIC: *As before.*

CROAK: Joe.

WORDS: [*As before.*] My Lord.

73

CROAK: Be friends! [*Pause.*] I am late, forgive. [*Pause.*] The face. [*Pause.*] On the stairs. [*Pause.*] Forgive. [*Pause.*] Joe.

WORDS: [*As before.*] My Lord.

CROAK: Bob.

MUSIC: *As before.*

CROAK: Forgive. [*Pause.*] In the tower. [*Pause.*] The face. [*Long pause.*] Theme tonight . . . [*Pause.*] Theme tonight . . . love. [*Pause.*] Love. [*Pause.*] My club. [*Pause.*] Joe.

WORDS: [*As before.*] My Lord.

CROAK: Love. [*Pause. Thump of club on ground.*] Love!

WORDS: [*Orotund.*] Love is of all the passions the most power- ful passion and indeed no passion is more powerful than the passion of love. [*Clears throat.*] This is the mode in which the mind is most strongly affected and indeed in no mode is the mind more strongly affected than in this. [*Pause.*]

CROAK: *Rending sigh. Thump of club.*

WORDS: [*As before.*] By passion we are to understand a move- ment of the mind pursuing or fleeing real or imagined pleasure or pain. [*Clears throat.*] Of all—

CROAK: [*Anguished.*] Oh!

WORDS: [*As before.*] Of all these movements then and who can number them and they are legion sloth is the LOVE is the most urgent and indeed by no manner of movement is the soul more urged than by this, to and—

[*Violent thump of club.*]

CROAK: Bob.

WORDS: From.

[*Violent thump of club.*]

CROAK: Bob.

MUSIC: *As before.*

CROAK: Love!

MUSIC: *Rap of baton on stand. Soft music worthy of foregoing, great expression, with audible groans and protestations—'No!'*'Please!' *etc.—from* WORDS. *Pause.*

CROAK: [*Anguished.*] Oh! [*Thump of club.*] Louder!

MUSIC: *Loud rap of baton and as before fortissimo, all expression gone, drowning* WORDS' *protestations. Pause.*

CROAK: My comforts! [*Pause.*] Joe sweet.

WORDS: [*As before.*] Arise then and go now the manifest unanswerable—

CROAK: *Groans.*

WORDS: —to wit this love what is this love that more than all the cursed deadly or any other of its great movers so moves the soul and soul what is this soul that more than by any of its great movers is by love so moved? [*Clears throat. Prosaic.*] Love of woman, I mean, if that is what my Lord means.

CROAK: Alas!

WORDS: What? [*Pause. Very rhetorical.*] Is love the word? [*Pause. Do.*] Is soul the word? [*Pause. Do.*] Do we mean love, when we say love? [*Pause. Pause. Do.*] Soul, when we say soul?

CROAK: [*Anguished.*] Oh! [*Pause.*] Bob dear.

WORDS: Do we? [*With sudden gravity.*] Or don't we?

CROAK: [*Imploring.*] Bob!

MUSIC: *Rap of baton. Love and soul music, with just audible protestations—'No!' 'Please!' 'Peace!' etc.—from* WORDS. *Pause.*

CROAK: [*Anguished.*] Oh! [*Pause.*] My balms! [*Pause.*] Joe.

WORDS: [*Humble.*] My Lord.

CROAK: Bob.

MUSIC: *Adsum as before.*

CROAK: My balms! [*Pause.*] Joe. [*Pause. Thump of club.*] Joe.

WORDS: [*As before.*] My Lord.

CROAK: Age!

[*Pause.*]

WORDS: [*Faltering.*] Age is . . . age is when . . . old age I mean . . . if that is what my Lord means . . . is when . . . if you're a man . . . were a man . . . huddled . . . nodding . . . the ingle . . . waiting—

[*Violent thump of club.*]

CROAK: Bob. [*Pause.*] Age. [*Pause. Violent thump of club.*] Age!

75

MUSIC: *Rap of baton. Age music, soon interrupted by violent thump.*

CROAK: Together. [*Pause. Thump.*] Together! [*Pause. Violent thump.*] Together, dogs!

MUSIC: *Long la.*

WORDS: [*Imploring.*] No!
[*Violent thump.*]

CROAK: Dogs!

MUSIC: *La.*

WORDS: [*Trying to sing.*] Age is when . . . to a man . . .

MUSIC: *Improvement of above.*

WORDS: [*Trying to sing this.*] Age is when to a man . .

MUSIC: *Suggestion for following.*

WORDS: [*Trying to sing this.*] Huddled o'er . . . the ingle . . . [*Pause. Violent thump. Trying to sing.*] Waiting for the hag to put the . . . pan in the bed . . .

MUSIC: *Improvement of above.*

WORDS: [*Trying to sing this.*] Waiting for the hag to put the pan in the bed.

MUSIC: *Suggestion for following.*

WORDS: [*Trying to sing this.*] And bring the . . . arrowroot . . . [*Pause. Violent thump. As before.*] And bring the toddy . . .
[*Pause. Tremendous thump.*]

CROAK: Dogs!

MUSIC: *Suggestion for following.*

WORDS: [*Trying to sing this.*] She comes in the ashes . . . [*Imploring.*] No!

MUSIC: *Repeats suggestion.*

WORDS: [*Trying to sing this.*] She comes in the ashes who loved could not be . . . won or . . .
[*Pause.*]

MUSIC: *Repeats end of previous suggestion.*

WORDS: [*Trying to sing this.*] Or won not loved . . . [*Wearily.*] . . . or some other trouble . . . [*Pause. Trying to sing.*]
Comes in the ashes like in that old—

MUSIC: *Interrupts with improvement of this and brief suggestion.*

WORDS: [*Trying to sing this.*] Comes in the ashes like in that old light . . . her face . . . in the ashes . . .

   [*Pause.*]

CROAK: *Groans.*

MUSIC: *Suggestion for following.*

WORDS: [*Trying to sing this.*] That old moonlight . . . on the earth . . . again.

   [*Pause.*]

MUSIC: *Further brief suggestion.*

   [*Silence.*]

CROAK: *Groans.*

MUSIC: *Plays air through alone, then invites* WORDS *with opening, pause, invites again and finally accompanies very softly.*

WORDS: [*Trying to sing, softly.*]

> Age is when to a man
> Huddled o'er the ingle
> Shivering for the hag
> To put the pan in the bed
> And bring the toddy
> She comes in the ashes
> Who loved could not be won
> Or won not loved
> Or some other trouble
> Comes in the ashes
> Like in that old light
> The face in the ashes
> That old starlight
> On the earth again.

   [*Long pause.*]

CROAK: [*Murmur.*] The face. [*Pause.*] The face. [*Pause.*] The face. [*Pause.*] The face.

MUSIC: *Rap of baton and warmly sentimental, about one minute.*

   [*Pause.*]

CROAK: The face.

WORDS: [*Cold.*] Seen from above in that radiance so cold and faint . . .
    [*Pause.*]

MUSIC: *Warm suggestion from above for above.*

WORDS: [*Disregarding, cold.*] Seen from above at such close quarters in that radiance so cold and faint with eyes so dimmed by . . . what had passed, its quite . . . piercing beauty is a little . . .
    [*Pause.*]

MUSIC: *Renews timidly previous suggestion.*

WORDS: [*Interrupting, violently.*] Peace!

CROAK: My comforts! Be friends!
    [*Pause.*]

WORDS: . . . blunted. Some moments later however, such are the powers of recuperation at this age, the head is drawn back to a distance of two or three feet, the eyes widen to a stare and begin to feast again. [*Pause.*] What then is seen would have been better seen in the light of day, that is incontestable. But how often it has, in recent months, how often, at all hours, under all angles, in cloud and shine, been seen I mean. And there is, is there not, in that clarity of silver . . . that clarity of silver . . . is there not . . . my Lord . . . [*Pause.*] Now and then the rye, swayed by a light wind, casts and withdraws its shadow.
    [*Pause.*]

CROAK: *Groans.*

WORDS: Leaving aside the features or lineaments proper, matchless severally and in their ordonnance—

CROAK: *Groans.*

WORDS: —flare of the black disordered hair as though spread wide on water, the brows knitted in a groove suggesting pain but simply concentration more likely all things considered on some consummate inner process, the eyes of course closed in keeping with this, the lashes . . . [*Pause.*] . . . the nose . . . [*Pause.*] . . . nothing, a little pinched perhaps, the lips . . .

78

CROAK: [*Anguished.*] Lily!

WORDS: . . . tight, a gleam of tooth biting on the under, no coral, no swell, whereas normally . . .

CROAK: *Groans.*

WORDS: . . . the whole so blanched and still that were it not for the great white rise and fall of the breasts, spreading as they mount and then subsiding to their natural . . . aperture—

MUSIC: *Irrepressible burst of spreading and subsiding music with vain protestations—'Peace!' 'No!' 'Please!' etc.—from* WORDS. *Triumph and conclusion.*

WORDS: [*Gently expostulatory.*] My Lord! [*Pause. Faint thump of club.*] I resume, so wan and still and so ravished away that it seems no more of the earth than Mira in the Whale, at her tenth and greatest magnitude on this particular night shining coldly down—as we say, looking up. [*Pause.*] Some moments later however, such are the powers—

CROAK: [*Anguished.*] No!

WORDS: —the brows uncloud, the lips part and the eyes . . . [*Pause.*] . . . the brows uncloud, the nostrils dilate, the lips part and the eyes . . . [*Pause.*] . . . a little colour comes back into the cheeks and the eyes . . . [*Reverently.*] . . . open. [*Pause.*] Then down a little way . . . [*Pause. Change to poetic tone. Low.*]

> Then down a little way
> Through the trash
> To where . . . towards where . . .

[*Pause.*]

MUSIC: *Discreet suggestion for above.*

WORDS: [*Trying to sing this.*]

> Then down a little way
> Through the trash
> Towards where . . .

[*Pause.*]

MUSIC: *Discreet suggestion for following.*

WORDS: [*Trying to sing this.*]

> All dark no begging
> No giving no words
> No sense no need . . .

[*Pause.*]

MUSIC: *More confident suggestion for following.*

WORDS: [*Trying to sing this.*]

> Through the scum
> Down a little way
> To where one glimpse
> Of that wellhead.

[*Pause.*]

MUSIC: *Invites with opening, pause, invites again and finally accompanies very softly.*

WORDS: [*Trying to sing, softly.*]

> Then down a little way
> Through the trash
> Towards where
> All dark no begging
> No giving no words
> No sense no need
> Through the scum
> Down a little way
> To whence one glimpse
> Of that wellhead.

[*Pause. Shocked.*] My Lord! [*Sound of club let fall. As before.*] My Lord! [*Shuffling slippers, with halts. They die away. Long pause.*] Bob. [*Pause.*] Bob!

MUSIC: *Brief rude retort.*

WORDS: Music. [*Imploring.*] Music!

[*Pause.*]

MUSIC: *Rap of baton and statement with elements already used or wellhead alone.*

[*Pause.*]

WORDS: Again. [*Pause. Imploring.*] Again!
MUSIC: *As before or only very slightly varied.*
    [*Pause.*]
WORDS: *Deep sigh.*

END

Cascando

A radio piece for music and voice

Written in French in 1962, with music by Marcel Mihalovici. First broadcast in English on the BBC Third Programme on 6 October 1964. First published in English in *Evergreen Review* (May/June 1963).

OPENER
VOICE
MUSIC

OPENER: [*Cold.*] It is the month of May . . . for me.

[*Pause.*]

Correct.

[*Pause.*]

I open.

VOICE: [*Low, panting.*] —story . . . if you could finish it . . . you could rest . . . sleep . . . not before . . . oh I know . . . the ones I've finished . . . thousands and one . . . all I ever did . . . in my life . . . with my life . . . saying to myself . . . finish this one . . . it's the right one . . . then rest . . . sleep . . . no more stories . . . no more words . . . and finished it . . . and not the right one . . . couldn't rest . . . straight away another . . . to begin . . . to finish . . . saying to myself . . . finish this one . . . then rest . . . this time . . . it's the right one . . . this time . . . you have it . . . and finished it . . . and not the right one . . . couldn't rest . . . straight away another . . . but this one . . . it's different . . . I'll finish it . . . I've got it . . . Woburn . . . I resume . . . a long life . . . already . . . say what you like . . . a few misfortunes . . . that's enough . . . five years later . . . ten . . . I don't know . . . Woburn . . . he's changed . . . not enough . . . recognizable . . . in the shed . . . yet another . . . waiting for night . . . night to fall . . . to go out . . . go on . . . elsewhere . . . sleep elsewhere . . . it's slow . . . he lifts his head . . . now and then . . . his eyes . . . to the window . . . it's darkening . . . earth darkening . . . it's night . . . he gets up . . . knees first . . . then up . . . on his feet . . . slips out . . . Woburn . . . same old coat . . . right the sea . . . left the hills . . . he has the choice . . . he has only—

OPENER: [*With* VOICE.] And I close.

85

[*Silence.*]

I open the other.

MUSIC: . . . .

OPENER: [*With* MUSIC.] And I close.

[*Silence.*]

I open both.

VOICE: ⎤
      ⎬ [*Together*]   —on . . . getting on . . . finish . . . don't
MUSIC: ⎦   . . . .

give up . . . then rest . . . sleep . . . not before . . . finish . . .

. . . .

this time . . . it's the right one . . . you have it . . . you've got

. . . .

it . . . it's there . . . somewhere . . . you've got him . . . follow

. . . .

him . . . don't lose him . . . Woburn story . . . getting on

. . . .

finish . . . then sleep . . . no more stories . . . no more

words . . . .

. . . come on . . . next thing . . . he—

. . . .

OPENER: [*With* VOICE *and* MUSIC.] And I close.

[*Silence.*]

I start again.

VOICE: —down . . . gentle slopes . . . boreen . . . giant aspens
. . . wind in the boughs . . . faint sea . . . Woburn . . . same
old coat . . . he goes on . . . stops . . . not a soul . . . not yet
. . . night too bright . . . say what you like . . . he goes
on . . . hugging the bank . . . same old stick . . . he goes
down . . . falls . . . on purpose or not . . . can't see . . . he's
down . . . that's what counts . . . face in the mud . . . arms
spread . . . that's the idea . . . already . . . there already . . .
no not yet . . . he gets up . . . knees first . . . hands flat . . .
in the mud . . . head sunk . . . then up . . . on his feet . . .
huge bulk . . . come on . . . he goes on . . . he goes down
. . . come on . . . in his head . . . what's in his head . . . a
hole . . . a shelter . . . a hollow . . . in the dunes . . . a cave

... vague memory ... in his head ... of a cave ... he goes down ... no more trees ... no more bank ... he's changed ... not enough ... night too bright ... soon the dunes ... no more cover ... not a soul ... not—

[*Silence.*]

MUSIC: ....

[*Silence.*]

VOICE: ⎤
     ⎥ [*Together*]   —rest ... sleep ... no more stories ...
MUSIC: ⎦ ....

no more words ... don't give up ... this time ... it's the
....
right one ... we're there ... I'm there ... somewhere ...
....
Woburn ... I've got him ... don't lose him ... follow him
....
... to the end ... come on ... this time ... it's the right one
....
... finish ... sleep ... Woburn ... come on—
....

[*Silence.*]

OPENER: So, at will.

They say, It's in his head.

No. I open.

VOICE: —falls ... again ... on purpose or not ... can't see ... he's down ... that's what matters ... face in the sand ... arms spread ... bare dunes ... not a scrub ... same old coat ... night too bright ... say what you like ... sea louder ... thunder ... manes of foam ... Woburn ... his head ... what's in his head ... peace ... peace again ... in his head ... no further ... no more searching ... sleep ... no not yet ... he gets up ... knees first ... hands flat ... in the sand ... head sunk ... then up ... on his feet ... huge bulk ... same old broadbrim ... jammed down ... come on ... he goes on ... ton weight ... in the sand ... knee-deep ... he goes down ... sea—

OPENER: [*With* VOICE.] And I close.

    [*Silence.*]

    I open the other.

MUSIC: . . . .

OPENER: [*With* MUSIC.] And I close.

    [*Silence.*]

    So, at will.

    It's my life, I live on that.

    [*Pause.*]

    Correct.

    [*Pause.*]

    What do I open?

    They say, He opens nothing, he has nothing to open, it's in his head.

    They don't see me, they don't see what I do, they don't see what I have, and they say, He opens nothing, he has nothing to open, it's in his head.

    I don't protest any more, I don't say any more,

    There is nothing in my head.

    I don't answer any more.

    I open and close.

VOICE: —lights . . . of the land . . . the island . . . the sky . . . he need only . . . lift his head . . . his eyes . . . he'd see them . . . shine on him . . . but no . . . he—

    [*Silence.*]

MUSIC: [*Brief.*]. . . . .

    [*Silence.*]

OPENER: They say, That is not his life, he does not live on that.

    They don't see me, they don't see what my life is, they don't see what I live on, and they say, That is not his life, he does not live on that.

    [*Pause.*]

    I have lived on it . . . till I'm old.

    Old enough.

    Listen.

VOICE: [*Weakening.*] —this time . . . I'm there . . . Woburn . . . it's him . . . I've seen him . . . I've got him . . . come on . . . same old coat . . . he goes down . . . falls . . . falls again . . . on purpose or not . . . can't see . . . he's down . . . that's what counts . . . come on—

OPENER: [*With* VOICE.] Full strength.

VOICE: —face . . . in the stones . . . no more sand . . . all stones . . . that's the idea . . . we're there . . . this time . . . no not yet . . . he gets up . . . knees first . . . hands flat . . . in the stones . . . head sunk . . . then up . . . on his feet . . . huge bulk . . . Woburn . . . faster . . . he goes on . . . he goes down . . . he—
[*Silence.*]

MUSIC: [*Weakening.*] . . . .

OPENER: [*With* MUSIC.] Full strength.

MUSIC: . . . .
[*Silence.*]

OPENER: That's not all.

I open both.

Listen.

VOICE: ⎤
MUSIC: ⎦ [*Together.*] —sleep . . . no further . . . no more
. . . .

searching . . . to find him . . . in the dark . . . to see him . . .
. . . .

to say him . . . for whom . . . that's it . . . no matter . . .
. . . .

never him . . . never right . . . start again . . . in the dark
. . . .

done with that . . . this time . . . it's the right one . . . we're
. . . .

there . . . nearly . . . finish—
. . . .
[*Silence.*]

OPENER: From one world to another, it's as though they drew together. We have not much further to go. Good.

VOICE: ⎤ [*Together.*]   —nearly . . . I've got him . . . I've seen
MUSIC: ⎦   . . . .

him . . . I've said him . . . we're there . . . nearly . . . no more
. . . .
stories . . . all false . . . this time . . . it's the right one . . . I
. . . .
have it . . . finish . . . sleep . . . Woburn . . . it's him . . . I've
. . . .
got him . . . follow him . . . to—

. . . .
[*Silence.*]

OPENER: Good.
[*Pause.*]
Yes, correct, the month of May.
You know, the reawakening.
[*Pause.*]
I open.

VOICE: —no tiller . . . no thwarts . . . no oars . . . afloat . . .
sucked out . . . then back . . . aground . . . drags free . . .
out . . . Woburn . . . he fills it . . . flat out . . . face in the
bilge . . . arms spread . . . same old coat . . . hands clutching . . . the gunnels . . . no . . . I don't know . . . I see him
. . . he clings on . . . out to sea . . . heading nowhere . . . for
the island . . . then no more . . . else—
[*Silence.*]

MUSIC: . . . .
[*Silence.*]

OPENER: They said, It's his own, it's his voice, it's in his head.
[*Pause.*]

VOICE: —faster . . . out . . . driving out . . . rearing . . . plunging
. . . heading nowhere . . . for the island . . . then no
more . . . elsewhere . . . anywhere . . . heading anywhere
. . . lights—
[*Pause.*]

OPENER: No resemblance.
I answered, And that . . .

MUSIC: [*Brief.*] . . . .
    [*Silence.*]

OPENER: . . . is that mine too?
    But I don't answer any more.
    And they don't say anything any more.
    They have quit.
    Good.
    [*Pause.*]
    Yes, correct, the month of May, the close of May.
    The long days.
    [*Pause.*]
    I open.
    [*Pause.*]
    I'm afraid to open.
    But I must open.
    So I open.

VOICE: —come on . . . Woburn . . . arms spread . . . same old
    coat . . . face in the bilge . . . he clings on . . . island gone
    . . . far astern . . . heading out . . . open sea . . . land gone
    . . . his head . . . what's in his head . . . Woburn—

OPENER: [*With* VOICE.] Come on! Come on!

VOICE: —at last . . . we're there . . . no further . . . no more
    searching . . . in the dark . . . elsewhere . . . always else-
    where . . . we're there . . . nearly . . . Woburn . . . hang on
    . . . don't let go . . . lights gone . . . of the land . . . all
    gone . . . nearly all . . . too far . . . too late . . . of the
    sky . . . those . . . if you like . . . he need only . . . turn
    over . . . he'd see them . . . shine on him . . . but no . . .
    he clings on . . . Woburn . . . he's changed . . . nearly
    enough—
    [*Silence.*]

MUSIC: . . . .

OPENER: [*With* MUSIC.] God.

MUSIC: . . . .
    [*Silence.*]

OPENER: God God.

[*Pause.*]

There was a time I asked myself, What is it.

There were times I answered, It's the outing.

Two outings.

Then the return.

Where?

To the village.

To the inn.

Two outings, then at last the return, to the village, to the inn, by the only road that leads there.

An image, like any other.

But I don't answer any more.

I open.

VOICE: ⎤
⎟ [*Together.*] —don't let go . . . finish . . . it's the
MUSIC: ⎦ . . . .

right one . . . this time . . . I have it . . . we're there . . .

. . . .

Woburn . . . nearly—

. . . .

OPENER: [*With* VOICE *and* MUSIC.] As though they had linked their arms.

VOICE: ⎤
⎟ [*Together.*] —sleep . . . no more stories . . . come on
MUSIC: ⎦ . . . .

. . . Woburn . . . it's him . . . see him . . . say him . . . to the

. . . .

end . . . don't let go—

OPENER: [*With* VOICE *and* MUSIC.] Good.

VOICE: ⎤
⎟ [*Together.*] —nearly . . . just a few more . . . a few
MUSIC: ⎦ . . . .

more . . . I'm there . . . nearly . . . Woburn . . . it's him . . . it

. . . .

was him . . . I've got him . . . nearly—

OPENER: [*With* VOICE *and* MUSIC, *fervently.*] Good!

VOICE: ⎤
⎟ [*Together.*] —this time . . . it's the right one . . .
MUSIC: ⎦ . . . .

finish . . . no more stories . . . sleep . . . we're there . . . nearly

. . . .
. . . just a few more . . . don't let go . . . Woburn . . . he clings
. . . .
on . . . come on . . . come on—
. . . .
[*Silence.*]

END

Film

Written in English in April 1963. First shown publicly at the New York Film Festival in 1965. First published by Faber and Faber in 1967.

Throughout first two parts all perception is E's. E is the camera. But in third part there is O's perception of room and contents and at the same time E's continued perception of O. This poses a problem of images which I cannot solve without technical help. See below, note 8.

The film is divided into three parts. 1. The street (about eight minutes). 2. The stairs (about five minutes). 3. The room (about seventeen minutes).

The film is entirely silent except for the "sssh!" in part one.

Climate of film comic and unreal. O should invite laughter throughout by his way of moving. Unreality of street scene (see notes to this section).

GENERAL

Esse est percipi.

All extraneous perception suppressed, animal, human, divine, self-perception maintains in being.

Search of non-being in flight from extraneous perception breaking down in inescapability of self-perception.

No truth value attaches to above, regarded as of merely structural and dramatic convenience.

In order to be figured in this situation the protagonist is sundered into object (O) and eye (E), the former in flight, the latter in pursuit.

It will not be clear until end of film that pursuing perceiver is not extraneous, but self.

Until end of film O is perceived by E from behind and at an angle not exceeding 45°. Convention: O enters *percipi* = experiences anguish of perceivedness, only when this angle is exceeded.

O not in perceivedness:

O in perceivedness:

E is therefore at pains, throughout pursuit, to keep within this 'angle of immunity' and only exceeds it (1) inadvertently at beginning of part one when he first sights O (2) inadvertently at beginning of part two when he follows O into vestibule and (3) deliberately at end of part three when O is cornered. In first two cases he hastily reduces angle.

OUTLINE

1. The street:

Dead straight. No sidestreets or intersections. Period: about 1929. Early summer morning. Small factory district. Moderate animation of workers going unhurriedly to work. All going in same direction and all in couples. No automobiles. Two bicycles ridden by men with girl passengers (on crossbar). One cab, cantering nag, driver standing brandishing whip. All persons in opening scene to be shown in some way perceiving—one another, an object, a shop window, a poster, etc., i.e. all contentedly in *percipere* and *percipi*. First view of above is by E motionless and searching with his eyes for O. He may be supposed at street edge of wide (four yards) sidewalk. O finally comes into view hastening blindly along sidewalk, hugging the wall on his left, in opposite direction to all the others. Long dark overcoat (whereas all others in light summer dress) with collar up, hat pulled down over eyes, briefcase in left hand, right hand

98

shielding exposed side of face. He storms along in comic foundered precipitancy. E's searching eye, turning left from street to sidewalk, picks him up at an angle exceeding that of immunity (O's unperceivedness according to convention) (1). O, entering perceivedness, reacts (after just sufficient onward movement for his gait to be established) by halting and cringing aside towards wall. E immediately draws back to close the angle (2) and O, released from perceivedness, hurries on. E lets him get about ten yards ahead and then starts after him (3). Street elements from now on incidental (except for episode of couple) in the sense that only registered in so far as they happen to enter field of pursuing eye fixed on O.

Episode of couple (4). In his blind haste O jostles an elderly couple of shabby genteel aspect, standing on sidewalk, peering together at a newspaper. They should be discovered by E a few yards before collision. The woman is holding a pet monkey under her left arm. E follows O an instant as he hastens blindly on, then registers couple recovering from shock, comes up with them, passes them slightly and halts to observe them (5). Having recovered they turn and look after O, the woman raising a lorgnon to her eyes, the man taking off his pince-nez fastened to his coat by a ribbon. They then look at each other, she lowering her lorgnon, he resuming his pince-nez. He opens his mouth to vituperate. She checks him with a gesture and soft "sssh!" He turns again, taking off his pince-nez, to look after O. She feels the gaze of E upon them and turns, raising her lorgnon, to look at him. She nudges her companion who turns back towards her, resuming his pince-nez, follows direction of her gaze and, taking off his pince-nez, looks at E. As they both stare at E the expression gradually comes over their faces which will be that of the flower-woman in the stairs scene and that of O at the end of film, an expression only to be described as corresponding to an agony of perceivedness. Indifference of monkey, looking up into face of its mistress. They close their eyes, she lowering her lorgnon, and hasten away in direction of all the others, i.e. that opposed to O and E (6).

E turns back towards O by now far ahead and out of sight. Immediate acceleration of E in pursuit (blurred transit of encountered elements). O comes into view, grows rapidly larger until E settles down behind him at same angle and remove as before. O disappears suddenly through open housedoor on his left. Immediate acceleration of E who comes up with O in vestibule at foot of stairs.

2. Stairs:

Vestibule about four yards square with stairs at inner righthand angle. Relation of streetdoor to stairs such that E's first perception of O (E near door, O motionless at foot of stairs, right hand on banister, body shaken by panting) is from an angle a little exceeding that of immunity. O, entering perceivedness (according to convention), transfers right hand from banister to exposed side of face and cringes aside towards wall on his left. E immediately draws back to close the angle and O, released, resumes his pose at foot of stairs, hand on banister. O mounts a few steps (E remaining near door), raises head, listens, redescends hastily backwards and crouches down in angle of stairs and wall on his right, invisible to one descending (7). E registers him there, then transfers to stairs. A frail old woman appears on bottom landing. She carries a tray of flowers slung from her neck by a strap. She descends slowly, with fumbling feet, one hand steadying the tray, the other holding the banister. Absorbed by difficulty of descent she does not become aware of E until she is quite down and making for the door. She halts and looks full at E. Gradually same expression as that of couple in street. She closes her eyes, then sinks to the ground and lies with face in scattered flowers. E lingers on this a moment, then transfers to where O last registered. He is no longer there, but hastening up the stairs. E transfers to stairs and picks up O as he reaches first landing. Bound forwards and up of E who overtakes O on second flight and is literally at his heels when he reaches second landing and opens with key door of room. They enter room together, E turning with O as he turns to lock the door behind him.

3. The room:

Here we assume problem of dual perception solved and enter O's perception (8). E must so manoeuvre throughout what follows, until investment proper, that O is always seen from behind, at most convenient remove, and from an angle never exceeding that of immunity, i.e. preserved from perceivedness.

Small barely furnished room (9). Side by side on floor a large cat and small dog. Unreal quality. Motionless till ejected. Cat bigger than dog. On a table against wall a parrot in a cage and a goldfish in a bowl. This room sequence falls into three parts.

1. Preparation of room (occlusion of window and mirror, ejection of dog and cat, destruction of God's image, occlusion of parrot and goldfish).

2. Period in rocking-chair. Inspection and destruction of photographs.

3. Final investment of O by E and dénouement.

Part 1. O stands near door with case in hand and takes in room. Succession of images: dog and cat, side by side, staring at him; mirror; window; couch with rug; dog and cat staring at him; parrot and goldfish, parrot staring at him; rocking-chair; dog and cat staring at him. He sets down case, approaches window from side and draws curtain. He turns towards dog and cat, still staring at him, then goes to couch and takes up rug. He turns towards dog and cat, still staring at him. Holding rug before him he approaches mirror from side and covers it with rug. He turns towards parrot and goldfish, parrot still staring at him. He goes to rocking-chair, inspects it from front. Insistent image of curiously carved headrest (10). He turns towards dog and cat still staring at him. He puts them out of room (11). He takes up case and is moving towards chair when rug falls from mirror.

He drops briefcase, hastens to wall between couch and mirror, follows walls past window, approaches mirror from side, picks up rug and, holding it before him, covers mirror with it again. He returns to briefcase, picks it up, goes to chair, sits down and is opening case when disturbed by print, pinned to wall before him, of the face of God the Father, the eyes staring at him severely. He sets down case on floor to his left, gets up and inspects print. Insistent image of wall, paper hanging off in strips (10). He tears print from wall, tears it in four, throws down the pieces and grinds them underfoot. He turns back to chair, image again of its curious headrest, sits down, image again of tattered wall-paper, takes case on his knees, takes out a folder, sets down case on floor to his left and is opening folder when disturbed by parrot's eye. He lays folder on case, gets up, takes off overcoat, goes to parrot, close up of parrot's eye, covers cage with coat, goes back to chair, image again of head-rest, sits down, image again of tattered wall-paper, takes up folder and is opening it when disturbed by fish's eye. He lays folder on case, gets up, goes to fish, close-up of fish's eye, extends coat to cover bowl as well as cage, goes back to chair, image again of headrest, sits down, image again of wall, takes up folder, takes off hat and lays it on case to his left. Scant hair or bald to facilitate identification of narrow black elastic encircling head.

When O sits up and back his head is framed in headrest which is a narrower extension of backrest. Throughout scene of inspection and destruction of photographs E may be supposed immediately behind chair looking down over O's left shoulder (12).

Part 2. O opens folder, takes from it a packet of photographs (13), lays folder on case and begins to inspect photographs. He inspects them in order 1 to 7. When he has finished with 1 he lays it on his knees, inspects 2, lays it on top of 1, and so on, so that when he has finished inspecting them all 1 will be at the bottom of the pile and 7—or rather 6, for he does not lay down 7—at the top. He gives about six seconds each to 1–4, about twice as long to 5 and 6 (trembling hands). Looking at 6 he touches with forefinger little girl's face. After six seconds of 7 he tears it in four and drops pieces on floor on his left. He takes up 6 from top of pile on his knees, looks at it again for about three seconds, tears it in four and drops pieces on floor to his left. So on for the others, looking at each again for about three seconds before tearing it up. 1 must be on tougher mount for he has difficulty in tearing it across. Straining hands. He finally succeeds, drops pieces on floor and sits, rocking slightly, hands holding armrests (14).

Part 3. Investment proper. Perception from now on, if dual perception feasible, E's alone, except perception of E by O at end. E moves a little back (image of headrest from back), then starts circling to his left, approaches maximum angle and halts. From this open angle, beyond which he will enter *percipi*, O can be seen beginning to doze off. His visible hand relaxes on armrest, his head nods and falls forward, the rock approaches stillness. E advances, opening angle beyond limit of immunity, his gaze pierces the light sleep and O starts awake. The start revives the rock, immediately arrested by foot to floor. Tension of hand on armrest. Turning his head to right, O cringes away from perceivedness. E draws back to reduce the angle and after a moment, reassured, O turns back front and resumes his pose. The rock resumes, dies down slowly as O dozes off again. E now begins a much wider encirclement. Images of curtained window, walls and shrouded mirror to indicate his path and that he is not yet looking at O. Then brief image of O seen by E from well beyond the angle of immunity, i.e. from near the table with shrouded bowl and cage. O is now seen to be fast asleep, his head sunk on his chest and his hands, fallen from the armrests, limply dangling. E resumes his cautious approach. Images of shrouded bowl and cage and tattered wall adjoining, with same indication as before. Halt and brief image, not far short of fullface, of O still fast asleep. E advances last few yards along tattered wall and halts directly in front of O. Long image of O, full-face, against ground of headrest, sleeping. E's gaze pierces the sleep, O starts awake, stares up at E. Patch over O's left eye now seen for the first time. Rock revived by start, stilled at once by foot to ground. Hand clutches armrests. O half starts from chair, then stiffens, staring up at E. Gradually that look. Cut to E, of whom this very first image (face only, against ground of tattered wall). It is O's face (with patch) but with very different expression, impossible to describe, neither severity nor benignity, but rather acute *intentness*. A big nail is visible near left temple (patch side). Long image of the unblinking gaze. Cut back to O, still half risen, staring up, with that look. O closes his eyes and falls back in chair, starting off rock. He covers his face with his hands. Image of O rocking, his head in his hands but not yet bowed. Cut back to E. As before. Cut back to O. He sits, bowed forward, his head in his hands, gently rocking. Hold it as the rocking dies down.

END

NOTES

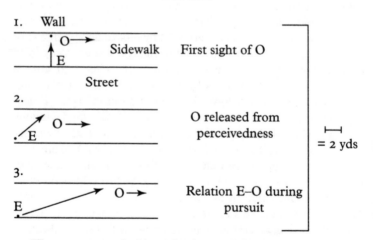

1. Wall
   O→ Sidewalk   First sight of O
   E
   Street

2.
   O→   O released from
   E   perceivedness

3.
   O→   Relation E–O during
   E   pursuit

⊢—⊣
= 2 yds

4. The purpose of this episode, undefendable except as a dramatic convenience, is to suggest as soon as possible unbearable quality of E's scrutiny. Reinforced by episode of flower-woman in stairs sequence.

5.

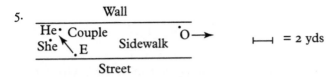

6. Expression of this episode, like that of animals' ejection in part three, should be as precisely stylized as possible. The purpose of the monkey, either unaware of E or indifferent to him, is to anticipate behaviour of animals in part three, attentive to O exclusively.

7. Suggestion for vestibule with (1) O in *percipi* (2) released (3) hiding from flower-woman. Note that even when E exceeds angle of immunity O's face never really seen because of immediate turn aside and (here) hand to shield face.

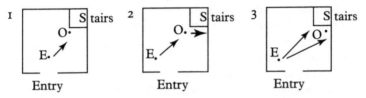

8. Up till now the perceptions of O, hastening *blindly* to illusory sanctuary, have been neglected and must in fact have been negligible. But in the room, until he falls asleep and the investment begins, they must be recorded. And at the same time E's perceiving of O must continue to be given. E is concerned only with O, not with the room, or only incidentally with the room in so far as its elements happen to enter the field of his gaze fastened on O. We see O in the room thanks to E's perceiving and the room itself thanks to O's perceiving. In other words this room sequence, up to the moment of O's falling asleep, is composed of two independent sets of images. I feel that any attempt to express them in simultaneity (composite images, double frame, superimposition, etc.) must prove unsatisfactory. The presentation in a single image of O's perception of the print, for example, and E's perception of O perceiving it—no

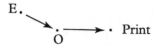

doubt feasible technically—would perhaps make impossible for the spectator a clear apprehension of either. The solution might be in a succession of images of different *quality*, corresponding on the one hand to E's perception of O and on the other to O's perception of the room. This difference of quality might perhaps be sought in different degrees of development, the passage from the one to the other being from greater to lesser and lesser to greater definition or luminosity. The dissimilarity, however obtained, would have to be flagrant. Having been up till now exclusively in the E quality, we would suddenly pass, with O's first survey of the room, into this quite different O quality. Then back to the E quality when O is shown moving to the window And so on throughout the sequence, switching from the one to the other as required. Were this the solution adopted it might be desirable to establish, by means of brief sequences, the O quality in parts one and two.

This seems to be the chief problem of the film, though I perhaps exaggerate its difficulty through technical ignorance.

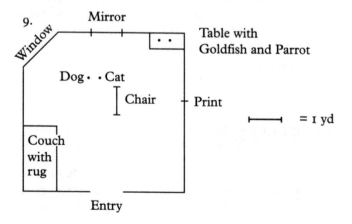

Suggestion for room.

This obviously cannot be O's room. It may be supposed it is his mother's room, which he has not visited for many years and is now to occupy momentarily, to look after the pets, until she comes out of hospital. This has no bearing on the film and need not be elucidated.

10. At close of film face E and face O can only be distinguished (1) By different expressions (2) by fact of O looking up and E down and (3) by difference of ground (for O headrest of chair, for E wall). Hence insistence on headrest and tattered wall.

11. Foolish suggestion for eviction of cat and dog. Also see Note 6.

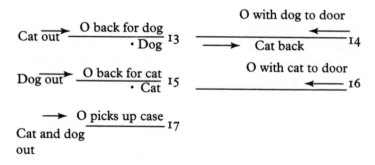

12. Chair from front during photo sequence.

13. Description of photographs.

1. Male infant. 6 months. His mother holds him in her arms. Infant smiles front. Mother's big hands. Her severe eyes devouring him. Her big old-fashioned beflowered hat.

2. The same. 4 years. On a veranda, dressed in loose nightshirt, kneeling on a cushion, attitude of prayer, hands clasped, head bowed, eyes closed. Half profile. Mother on chair beside him, big hands on knees, head bowed towards him, severe eyes, similar hat to 1.

3. The same. 15 years. Bareheaded. School blazer. Smiling. Teaching a dog to beg. Dog on its hind legs looking up at him.

4. The same. 20 years. Graduation day. Academic gown. Mortar-board under arm. On a platform, receiving scroll from Rector. Smiling. Section of public watching.

5. The same. 21 years. Bareheaded. Smiling. Small moustache. Arm round fiancée. A young man takes a snap of them.

6. The same. 25 years. Newly enlisted. Bareheaded. Uniform. Bigger moustache. Smiling. Holding a little girl in his arms. She looks into his face, exploring it with finger.

7. The same. 30 years. Looking over 40. Wearing hat and overcoat. Patch over left eye. Cleanshaven. Grim expression.

14. Profit by rocking-chair to emotionalize inspection, e.g. gentle steady rock for 1 to 4, rock stilled (foot to ground) after two seconds of 5, rock resumed between 5 and 6, rock stilled after two seconds of 6, rock resumed after 6 and for 7 as for 1–4.

Eh Joe

A piece for television

Written in English in April–May 1965. First broadcast on German television (SDR) on 13 April 1966. First published by Faber and Faber in 1967.

Joe: Late fifties, grey hair, old dressing-gown, carpet slippers, in his room.

1. Joe seen from behind sitting on edge of bed, intent pose, getting up, going to window, opening window, looking out, closing window, drawing curtain, standing intent.

2. Joe do. (=from behind) going from window to door, opening door, looking out, closing door, locking door, drawing hanging before door, standing intent.

3. Joe do. going from door to cupboard, opening cupboard, looking in, closing cupboard, locking cupboard, drawing hanging before cupboard, standing intent.

4. Joe do. going from cupboard to bed, kneeling down, looking under bed, getting up, sitting down on edge of bed as when discovered, beginning to relax.

5. Joe seen from front sitting on edge of bed, relaxed, eyes closed. Hold, then dolly slowly in to close-up of face. First word of text stops this movement.

Camera:

Joe's opening movements followed by camera at constant remove, Joe full length in frame throughout. No need to record room as whole. After this opening pursuit, between first and final closeup of face, camera has nine slight moves in towards face, say four inches each time. Each move is stopped by voice resuming, never camera move and voice together. This would give position of camera when dolly stopped by first word of text as one yard from maximum closeup of face. Camera does not move between paragraphs till clear that pause (say three seconds) longer than between phrases. Then four inches in say four seconds when movement stopped by voice resuming.

Voice:
Low, distinct, remote, little colour, absolutely steady rhythm, slightly slower than normal. Between phrases a beat of one second at least. Between paragraphs about seven, i.e. three before camera starts to advance and four for advance before it is stopped by voice resuming.

Face:
Practically motionless throughout, eyes unblinking during paragraphs, impassive except in so far as it reflects mounting tension of *listening*. Brief zones of relaxation between paragraphs when perhaps voice has relented for the evening and intentness may relax variously till restored by voice resuming.

WOMAN'S VOICE:
  Joe . . .
  [*Eyes open, resumption of intentness.*]
  Joe . . .
  [*Full intentness.*]
  Thought of everything? . . . Forgotten nothing? . . . You're all right now, eh? . . . No one can see you now . . . No one can get at you now . . . Why don't you put out that light? . . . There might be a louse watching you . . . Why don't you go to bed? . . . What's wrong with that bed, Joe? . . . You changed it, didn't you? . . . Made no difference? . . . Or is the heart already? . . . Crumbles when you lie down in the dark . . . Dry rotten at last . . . Eh Joe?

Camera move 1

  The best's to come, you said, that last time . . . Hurrying me into my coat . . . Last I was favoured with from you . . . Say it you now, Joe, no one'll hear you . . . Come on, Joe, no one can say it like you, say it again now and listen to yourself . . . The best's to come . . . You were right for once . . . In the end.

Camera move 2

You know that penny farthing hell you call your mind . . .
That's where you think this is coming from, don't you? . . .
That's where you heard your father . . . Isn't that what you
told me? . . . Started in on you one June night and went on
for years . . . On and off . . . Behind the eyes . . . That's
how you were able to throttle him in the end . . . Mental
thuggee you called it . . . One of your happiest fancies . . .
Mental thuggee . . . Otherwise he'd be plaguing you yet . . .
Then your mother when her hour came . . . 'Look up, Joe,
look up, we're watching you' . . . Weaker and weaker till
you laid her too . . . Others . . . All the others . . . Such
love he got . . . God knows why . . . Pitying love . . . None
to touch it . . . And look at him now . . . Throttling the
dead in his head.

Camera move 3

Anyone living love you now, Joe? . . . Anyone living sorry
for you now? . . . That slut that comes on Saturday, you
pay her, don't you? . . . Penny a hoist tuppence as long as
you like . . . Watch yourself you don't run short, Joe . . .
Ever think of that? . . . Eh Joe? . . . What it'd be if you ran
out of us . . . Not another soul to still . . . Sit there in his
stinking old wrapper hearing himself . . . That lifelong
adorer . . . Weaker and weaker till not a gasp left there
either . . . Is it that you want? . . . Well preserved for his
age and the silence of the grave . . . That old paradise
you were always harping on . . . No Joe . . . Not for the
likes of us.

Camera move 4

I was strong myself when I started . . . In on you . . .
Wasn't I, Joe? . . . Normal strength . . . Like those summer

evenings in the Green . . . In the early days . . . Of our idyll
. . . When we sat watching the ducks . . . Holding hands
exchanging vows . . . How you admired my elocution . . .
Among other charms . . . Voice like flint glass . . . To
borrow your expression . . . Powerful grasp of language you
had . . . Flint glass . . . You could have listened to it for
ever . . . And now this . . . Squeezed down to this . . . How
much longer would you say? . . . Till the whisper . . . you
know . . . when you can't hear the words . . . just the odd
one here and there . . . That's the worst . . . Isn't it, Joe?
. . . Isn't that what you told me . . . Before we expire . . .
The odd word . . . Straining to hear . . . Why must you do
that? . . . When you're nearly home . . . What matter then
. . . What we mean . . . It should be the best . . . Nearly
home again . . . Another stilled . . . And it's the worst . . .
Isn't that what you said? . . . The whisper . . . The odd
word . . . Straining to hear . . . Brain tired squeezing . . . It
stops in the end . . . You stop it in the end . . . Imagine if
you couldn't . . . Ever think of that? . . . If it went on . . .
The whisper in your head . . . Me whispering at you in
your head . . . Things you can't catch . . . On and off . . .
Till you join us . . . Eh Joe?

Camera move 5

How's your Lord these days? . . . Still worth having? . . .
Still lapping it up? . . . The passion of our Joe . . . Wait till
He starts talking to you . . . When you're done with yourself . . . All your dead dead . . . Sitting there in your foul
old wrapper . . . Very fair health for a man of your years . . .
Just that lump in your bubo . . . Silence of the grave
without the maggots . . . To crown your labours . . . Till
one night . . . 'Thou fool thy soul' . . . Put your thugs on
that . . . Eh Joe? . . . Ever think of that? . . . When He starts
in on you . . . When you're done with yourself . . . If you
ever are.

Camera move 6

Yes, great love God knows why . . . Even me . . . But I found a better . . . As I hope you heard . . . Preferable in all respects . . . Kinder . . . Stronger . . . More intelligent . . . Better looking . . . Cleaner . . . Truthful . . . Faithful . . . Sane . . . Yes . . . I did all right.

Camera move 7

But there was one didn't . . . You know the one I mean, Joe . . . The green one . . . The narrow one . . . Always pale . . . The pale eyes . . . Spirit made light . . . To borrow your expression . . . The way they opened after . . . Unique . . . Are you with me now? . . . Eh Joe? . . . There was love for you . . . The best's to come, you said . . . Bundling her into her Avoca sack . . . Her fingers fumbling with the big horn buttons . . . Ticket in your pocket for the first morning flight . . . You've had her, haven't you? . . . You've laid her? . . . Of course he has . . . She went young . . . No more old lip from her.

Camera move 8

Ever know what happened? . . . She didn't say? . . . Just the announcement in the *Independent* . . . 'On Mary's beads we plead her needs and in the Holy Mass' . . . Will I tell you? . . . Not interested? . . . Well I will just the same . . . I think you should know . . . That's right, Joe, squeeze away . . . Don't lose heart now . . . When you're nearly home . . . I'll soon be gone . . . The last of them . . . Unless that poor old slut loves you . . . Then yourself . . . That old bonfire . . . Years of that stink . . . Then the silence . . . A dollop of that . . . To crown all . . . Till His Nibs . . . One dirty winter night . . . 'Mud thou art.'

Camera move 9

All right . . . Warm summer night . . . All sleeping . . .
Sitting on the edge of her bed in her lavender slip . . . You
know the one . . . Ah she knew you, heavenly powers! . . .
Faint lap of sea through open window . . . Gets up in the
end and slips out as she is . . . Moon . . . Stock . . . Down
the garden and under the viaduct . . . Sees from the
seaweed the tide is flowing . . . Goes on down to the edge
and lies down with her face in the wash . . . Cut a long
story short doesn't work . . . Gets up in the end sopping
wet and back up to the house . . . Gets out the Gillette . . .
The make you recommended for her body hair . . . Back
down the garden and under the viaduct . . . Takes the
blade from the holder and lies down at the edge on her side
. . . Cut another long story short doesn't work either . . .
You know how she always dreaded pain . . . Tears a strip
from the slip and ties it round the scratch . . . Gets up in
the end and back up to the house . . . Slip clinging the way
wet silk will . . . This all new to you, Joe? . . . Eh Joe? . . .
Gets the tablets and back down the garden and under the
viaduct . . . Takes a few on the way . . . Unconscionable
hour by now . . . Moon going off the shore behind the hill
. . . Stands a bit looking at the beaten silver . . . Then starts
along the edge to a place further down near the Rock . . .
Imagine what in her mind to make her do that . . . Imagine
. . . Trailing her feet in the water like a child . . . Takes a
few more on the way . . . Will I go on, Joe? . . . Eh Joe? . . .
Lies down in the end with her face a few feet from the tide
. . . Clawing at the single now . . . Has it all worked out this
time . . . Finishes the tube . . . There's love for you . . . Eh
Joe? . . . Scoops a little cup for her face in the stones . . .
The green one . . . The narrow one . . . Always pale . . .
The pale eyes . . . The look they shed before . . . The way
they opened after . . . Spirit made light . . . Wasn't that
your description, Joe? . . .

[*Voice drops to whisper, almost inaudible except words in italics.*]

All right . . . You've had the best . . . Now *imagine* . . . Before she goes . . . Face in the cup . . . Lips on a *stone* . . . Taking Joe with her . . . Light gone . . . '*Joe Joe*' . . . No sound . . . To the *stones* . . . Say it you now, no one'll hear you . . . Say 'Joe' it parts the *lips* . . . *Imagine* the hands . . . The *solitaire* . . . Against a *stone* . . . Imagine the *eyes* . . . Spiritlight . . . Month of June . . . What year of your Lord? . . . *Breasts* in the stones . . . And the *hands* . . . Before they go . . . *Imagine* the hands . . . What are they at? . . . In the *stones* . . .

[*Image fades, voice as before.*]

What are they fondling? . . . Till they go . . . *There's love for you* . . . Isn't it, Joe? . . . Wasn't it, Joe? . . . *Eh Joe?* . . . Wouldn't you say? . . . Compared to us . . . Compared to Him . . . *Eh Joe?* . . .

[*Voice and image out.*]

END

Ghost Trio

A play for television

Written in English in 1975–6. First televised on BBC2 on 17 April 1977. First published by Grove Press (New York) in 1976.

v: Female voice
F: Male Figure

I   Pre-action
II   Action
III Re-action

Room: 6m. × 5m.

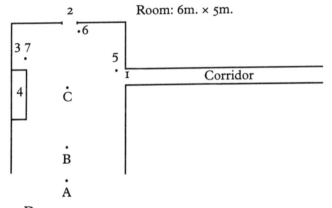

1 Door.
2 Window.
3 Mirror.
4 Pallet.
5 F seated by door.
6 F at window.
7 F at head of pallet.

A Position general view.
B Position medium shot.
C Position near shot of 5 and 1, 6 and 2, 7 and 3.

MUSIC

From Largo of Beethoven's Fifth Piano Trio Op. 70, No. 1 (*The Ghost*):

I.13	*beginning bar* 47
I.23	*beginning bar* 49
I.31–34	*beginning bar* 19
II.26–29	*beginning bar* 64
II.35–36	*beginning bar* 71
III.1–2, 4–5	*beginning bar* 26
III.29	*beginning bar* 64
III.36 end to	*beginning bar* 82

I

1. *Fade up to general view from A. 10 seconds.*
2. v: Good evening. Mine is a faint voice. Kindly tune accordingly. [*Pause.*] Good evening. Mine is a faint voice. Kindly tune accordingly. [*Pause.*] It will not be raised, nor lowered, whatever happens. [*Pause.*] Look. [*Long pause.*] The familiar chamber. [*Pause.*] At the far end a window. [*Pause.*] On the right the indispensable door. [*Pause.*] On the left, against the wall, some kind of pallet. [*Pause.*] The light: faint, omnipresent. No visible source. As if all luminous. Faintly luminous. No shadow. [*Pause.*] No shadow. Colour: none. All grey. Shades of grey. [*Pause.*] The colour grey if you wish, shades of the colour grey. [*Pause.*] Forgive my stating the obvious. [*Pause.*] Keep that sound down. [*Pause.*] Now look closer. [*Pause.*] Floor.
3. *Cut to close-up of floor. Smooth grey rectangle 0.70 m. × 1.50 m. 5 seconds.*
4. v: Dust. [*Pause.*] Having seen that specimen of floor you have seen it all. Wall.
5. *Cut to close-up of wall. Smooth grey rectangle 0.70 m. × 1.50 m. 5 seconds.*
6. v: Dust. [*Pause.*] Knowing this, the kind of wall—
7. *Close-up of wall continued. 5 seconds.*
8. v: The kind of floor—
9. *Cut to close-up of floor. 5 seconds.*
10. v: Look again.
11. *Cut to general view from A. 5 seconds.*
12. v: Door.
13. *Cut to close-up of whole door. Smooth grey rectangle 0.70 m. × 2 m. Imperceptibly ajar. No knob. Faint music. 5 seconds.*

14. v: Window.
15. *Cut to close-up of whole window. Opaque sheet of glass 0.70 m. × 1.50 m. Imperceptibly ajar. No knob. 5 seconds.*
16. v: Pallet.
17. *Cut to close-up from above of whole pallet. 0.70 m. × 2 m. Grey sheet. Grey rectangular pillow at window end. 5 seconds.*
18. v: Knowing all this, the kind of pallet—
19. *Close-up of whole pallet continued. 5 seconds.*
20. v: The kind of window—
21. *Cut to close-up of whole window. 5 seconds.*
22. v: The kind of door—
23. *Cut to close-up of whole door. Faint music. 5 seconds.*
24. v: The kind of wall—
25. *Cut to close-up of wall as before. 5 seconds.*
26. v: The kind of floor.
27. *Cut to close-up of floor as before. 5 seconds.*
28. v: Look again.
29. *Cut to general view. 5 seconds.*
30. v: Sole sign of life a seated figure.
31. *Move in slowly from A to B whence medium shot of F and door. F is seated on a stool, bowed forward, face hidden, clutching with both hands a small cassette not identifiable as such at this range. Faint music. 5 seconds.*
32. *Move in from B to C whence near shot of F and door. Cassette now identifiable. Music slightly louder, 5 seconds.*
33. *Move in from C to close-up of head, hands, cassette. Clutching hands, head bowed, face hidden. Music slightly louder. 5 seconds.*
34. *Move slowly back to A via C and B (no stops). Music progressively fainter till at level of B it ceases to be heard.*
35. *General view from A. 5 seconds.*

II

All from A except 26–29.

1. v: He will now think he hears her.
2. F *raises head sharply, turns still crouched to door, fleeting face, tense pose. 5 seconds.*
3. v: No one.
4. F *relapses into opening pose, bowed over cassette. 5 seconds.*
5. v: Again.
6. *Same as 2.*
7. v: Now to door.
8. F *gets up, lays cassette on stool, goes to door, listens with right ear against door, back to camera. 5 seconds.*
9. v: No one. [*Pause 5 seconds.*] Open.
10. *With right hand* F *pushes door open half-way clockwise, looks out, back to camera. 2 seconds.*
11. v: No one.
12. F *removes hand from door which closes slowly of itself, stands irresolute back to camera. 2 seconds.*
13. v: Now to window.
14. F *goes to window, stands irresolute, back to camera. 5 seconds.*
15. v: Open.
16. *With right hand* F *pushes window open half-way clockwise, looks out, back to camera. 5 seconds.*
17. v: No one.
18. F *removes hand from window which closes slowly of itself, stands irresolute, back to camera. 2 seconds.*
19. v: Now to pallet.
20. F *goes to head of pallet (window end), stands looking down at it. 5 seconds.*
21. F *turns to wall at head of pallet, goes to wall, looks at his face in mirror hanging on wall, invisible from A.*
22. v: [*Surprised.*] Ah!
23. *After 5 seconds* F *bows his head, stands before mirror with bowed head. 5 seconds.*
24. v: Now to door.

25. F *goes to stool, takes up cassette, sits, settles into opening pose, bowed over cassette. 5 seconds.*

26. *Same as I.31.*

27. *Same as I.32.*

28. *Same as I.33.*

29. *Same as I.34.*

30. *Same as I.35.*

31. v: He will now again think he hears her.

32. *Same as II.2.*

33. F *gets up, lays cassette on stool, goes to door, opens it as before, looks out, stoops forward. 10 seconds.*

34. F *straightens up, releases door which closes slowly of itself, stands irresolute, goes to stool, takes up cassette, sits irresolute, settles finally into opening pose, bowed over cassette. 5 seconds.*

35. *Faint music audible for first time at A. It grows louder. 5 seconds.*

36. v: Stop.

37. *Music stops. General view from A. 5 seconds.*

38. v: Repeat.

III

1. *Immediately after 'Repeat' cut to near shot from C of* F *and door. Music audible. 5 seconds.*
2. *Move in to close-up of head, hands, cassette. Music slightly louder. 5 seconds.*
3. *Music stops. Action II.2. 5 seconds.*
4. *Action II.4. Music resumes. 5 seconds.*
5. *Move back to near shot from C of* F *and door. Music audible. 5 seconds.*
6. *Music stops. Action II.2. Near shot from C of* F *and door. 5 seconds.*
7. *Action II.8. Near shot from C of stool, cassette,* F *with right ear to door. 5 seconds.*
8. *Action II.10. Crescendo creak of door opening. Near shot from C of stool, cassette,* F *with right hand holding door open. 5 seconds.*
9. *Cut to view of corridor seen from door. Long narrow (0.70 m.) grey rectangle between grey walls, empty, far end in darkness. 5 seconds.*
10. *Cut back to near shot from C of stool, cassette,* F *holding door open. 5 seconds.*
11. *Action II.12. Decrescendo creak of door slowly closing. Near shot from C of stool, cassette,* F *standing irresolute, door. 5 seconds.*
12. *Cut to close-up from above of cassette on stool, small grey rectangle on larger rectangle of seat. 5 seconds.*
13. *Cut back to near shot of stool, cassette,* F *standing irresolute, door. 5 seconds.*
14. *Action II.14 seen from C. Near shot from C of* F *and window. 5 seconds.*
15. *Action II.16 seen from C. Crescendo creak of window opening. Faint sound of rain. Near shot from C of* F *with right hand holding window open. 5 seconds.*
16. *Cut to view from window. Night. Rain falling in dim light. Sound of rain slightly louder. 5 seconds.*
17. *Cut back to near shot from C of* F *with right hand holding window open. Faint sound of rain. 5 seconds.*

18. *Action II.18 seen from C. Decrescendo creak of window slowly closing. Near shot from C of F and window. 5 seconds.*

19. *Action II.20 seen from C. Near shot from C of F, mirror, head of pallet.*

20. *Cut to close-up from above of whole pallet.*

21. *Move down to tighter close-up of pallet moving slowly from pillow to foot and back to pillow. 5 seconds on pillow.*

22. *Move back to close-up from above of whole pallet. 5 seconds.*

23. *Cut back to near shot from C of F, mirror, head of pallet. 5 seconds.*

24. *Cut to close-up of mirror reflecting nothing. Small grey rectangle (same dimensions as cassette) against larger rectangle of wall. 5 seconds.*

25. *Cut back to near shot from C of F, mirror, head of pallet. 5 seconds.*

26. *Action II.21 seen from C. Near shot from C of F and mirror. 5 seconds.*

27. *Cut to close-up of F's face in mirror. 5 seconds. Eyes close. 5 seconds. Eyes open. 5 seconds. Head bows. Top of head in mirror. 5 seconds.*

28. *Cut back to near shot from C of F with bowed head, mirror, head of pallet. 5 seconds.*

29. *Action II.25 seen from C. Near shot from C of F settling into opening pose. Music audible once settled. 10 seconds.*

30. *Music stops. Action II.2 seen from C. Faint sound of steps approaching. They stop. Faint sound of knock on door. 5 seconds. Second knock, no louder. 5 seconds.*

31. *Action II.33 seen from C. Crescendo creak of door slowly opening. Near shot from C of stool, cassette, F holding door open, stooping forward. 10 seconds.*

32. *Cut to near shot of small boy full length in corridor before open door. Dressed in black oilskin with hood glistening with rain. White face raised to invisible F. 5 seconds. Boy shakes head faintly. Face still, raised. 5 seconds. Boy shakes head again. Face still, raised. 5 seconds. Boy turns and goes. Sound of receding steps. Register from the same position his slow recession till he vanishes in dark at end of corridor. 5 seconds on empty corridor.*

33. *Cut back to near shot from C of stool, cassette, F holding door open. 5 seconds.*

34. *Action II.34 seen from C. Decrescendo creak of door slowly closing. 5 seconds.*

35. *Cut to general view from A. 5 seconds.*

36. *Music audible at A. It grows. 10 seconds.*

37. *With growing music move in slowly to close-up of head bowed right down over cassette now held in arms and invisible. Hold till end of Largo.*

38. *Silence. F raises head. Face seen clearly for second time. 10 seconds.*

39. *Move slowly back to A.*

40. *General view from A. 5 seconds.*

41. *Fade out.*

. . . but the clouds . . .

A play for television

Written in English in October–November 1976. First televised on BBC2 on 17 April 1977. First published by Faber and Faber in 1977.

M: Near shot from behind of man sitting on invisible stool bowed over invisible table. Light grey robe and skullcap. Dark ground. Same shot throughout.

MI: M in set. Hat and greatcoat dark, robe and skullcap light.

W: Close-up of woman's face reduced as far as possible to eyes and mouth. Same shot throughout.

S: Long shot of set empty or with MI. Same shot throughout.

V: M's voice.

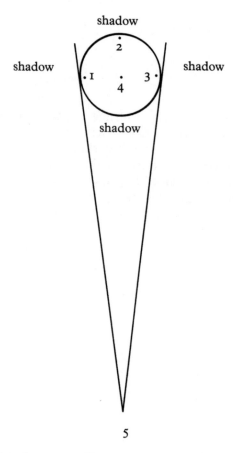

Set: circular, about 5 m. diameter, surrounded by deep shadow.

Lighting: a gradual lightening from dark periphery to maximum light at centre.

  1. West, roads.
  2. North, sanctum.
  3. East, closet.
  4. Standing position.
  5. Camera.

1. *Dark. 5 seconds.*
2. *Fade up to* M. *5 seconds.*
3. V: When I thought of her it was always night. I came in—
4. *Dissolve to* S *empty. 5 seconds.* MI *in hat and greatcoat emerges from west shadow, advances five steps and stands facing east shadow. 2 seconds.*
5. V: No—
6. *Dissolve to* M. *2 seconds.*
7. V: No, that is not right. When she appeared it was always night. I came in—
8. *Dissolve to* S *empty. 5 seconds.* MI *in hat and greatcoat emerges from west shadow, advances five steps and stands facing east shadow. 5 seconds.*
9. V: Right. Came in, having walked the roads since break of day, brought night home, stood listening [*5 seconds.*], finally went to closet—
10. MI *advances five steps to disappear in east shadow. 2 seconds.*
11. V: Shed my hat and greatcoat, assumed robe and skull, reappeared—
12. MI *in robe and skullcap emerges from east shadow, advances five steps and stands facing west shadow. 5 seconds.*
13. V: Reappeared and stood as before, only facing the other way, exhibiting the other outline [*5 seconds.*], finally turned and vanished—
14. MI *turns right and advances five steps to disappear in north shadow. 5 seconds.*
15. V: Vanished within my little sanctum and crouched, where none could see me, in the dark.
16. *Dissolve to* M. *5 seconds.*

17. V: Let us now make sure we have got it right.

18. *Dissolve to* S *empty. 2 seconds.* MI *in hat and greatcoat emerges from west shadow, advances five steps and stands facing east shadow. 2 seconds. He advances five steps to disappear in east shadow. 2 seconds. He emerges in robe and skullcap from east shadow, advances five steps and stands facing west shadow. 2 seconds. He turns right and advances five steps to disappear in north shadow. 2 seconds.*

19. V: Right.

20. *Dissolve to* M. *2 seconds.*

21. V: Then crouching there, in my little sanctum, in the dark, where none could see me, I began to beg, of her, to appear, to me. Such had long been my use and wont. No sound, a begging of the mind, to her, to appear, to me. Deep down into the dead of night, until I wearied, and ceased. Or of course until—

22. *Dissolve to* W. *2 seconds.*

23. *Dissolve to* M. *2 seconds.*

24. V: For had she never once appeared, all that time, would I have, could I have, gone on begging, all that time? Not just vanished within my little sanctum and busied myself with something else, or with nothing, busied myself with nothing? Until the time came, with break of day, to issue forth again, shed robe and skull, resume my hat and greatcoat, and issue forth again, to walk the roads.

25. *Dissolve to* S *empty. 2 seconds.* MI *in robe and skullcap emerges from north shadow, advances five steps and stands facing camera. 2 seconds. He turns left and advances five steps to disappear in east shadow. 2 seconds. He emerges in hat and greatcoat from east shadow, advances five steps and stands facing west shadow. 2 seconds. He advances five steps to disappear in west shadow. 2 seconds.*

26. V: Right.

27. *Dissolve to* M. *5 seconds.*

28. V: Let us now distinguish three cases. One: she appeared and—

29. *Dissolve to* W. *2 seconds.*

30. *Dissolve to* M. *2 seconds.*

31. V: In the same breath was gone. *2 seconds.* Two: she appeared and—

32. *Dissolve to* W. *5 seconds.*

33. V: Lingered. *5 seconds.* With those unseeing eyes I so begged when alive to look at me. *5 seconds.*

34. *Dissolve to* M. *2 seconds.*

35. V: Three: she appeared and—

36. *Dissolve to* W. *5 seconds.*

37. V: After a moment—

38. W's *lips move, uttering inaudibly:* '. . . clouds . . . but the clouds . . . of the sky . . .', V *murmuring, synchronous with lips:* '. . . but the clouds . . .' *Lips cease. 5 seconds.*

39. V: Right.

40. *Dissolve to* M. *5 seconds.*

41. V: Let us now run through it again.

42. *Dissolve to* S *empty. 2 seconds.* MI *in hat and greatcoat emerges from west shadow, advances five steps and stands facing east shadow. 2 seconds. He advances five steps to disappear in east shadow. 2 seconds. He emerges in robe and skullcap from east shadow, advances five steps and stands facing west shadow. 2 seconds. He turns right and advances five steps to disappear in north shadow. 2 seconds.*

43. *Dissolve to* M. *5 seconds.*

44. *Dissolve to* W. *2 seconds.*

45. *Dissolve to* M. *2 seconds.*

46. *Dissolve to* W. *5 seconds.*

47. V: Look at me. *5 seconds.*

48. *Dissolve to* M. *5 seconds.*

49. *Dissolve to* W. *2 seconds.* W's *lips move, uttering inaudibly:* '. . . clouds . . . but the clouds . . . of the sky . . .', V *murmuring, synchronous with lips:* '. . . but the clouds . . .' *Lips cease. 5 seconds.*

50. V: Speak to me. *5 seconds.*

51. *Dissolve to* M. *5 seconds.*

52. V: Right. There was of course a fourth case, or case nought, as I pleased to call it, by far the commonest, in the proportion say of nine hundred and ninety-nine to one, or nine hundred and ninety-eight to two, when I begged in vain, deep down into the dead of night, until I wearied, and ceased, and busied myself with something else, more ... rewarding, such as ... such as ... cube roots, for example, or with nothing, busied myself with nothing, that MINE, until the time came, with break of day, to issue forth again, void my little sanctum, shed robe and skull, resume my hat and greatcoat, and issue forth again, to walk the roads. [*Pause.*] The back roads.

53. *Dissolve to* S *empty. 2 seconds.* MI *in robe and skullcap emerges from north shadow, advances five steps and stands facing camera. 2 seconds. He turns left and advances five steps to disappear in east shadow. 2 seconds. He emerges in hat and greatcoat from east shadow, advances five steps and stands facing west shadow. 2 seconds. He advances five steps to disappear in west shadow. 2 seconds.*

54. V: Right.

55. *Dissolve to* M. *5 seconds.*

56. *Dissolve to* W. *5 seconds.*

57. V: '... but the clouds of the sky ... when the horizon fades ... or a bird's sleepy cry ... among the deepening shades ...' *5 seconds.*

58. *Dissolve to* M. *5 seconds.*

59. *Fade out on* M.

60. *Dark. 5 seconds.*

Quad

A piece for four players, light, and percussion.

Written in English in 1980–1. First broadcast on German television (SDR) on 8 October 1981. First published by Faber and Faber in 1984.

The players (1, 2, 3, 4) pace the given area, each following his particular course.

Area: Square. Length of side: 6 paces.

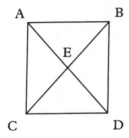

Course 1: AC, CB, BA, AD, DB, BC, CD, DA
Course 2: BA, AD, DB, BC, CD, DA, AC, CB
Course 3: CD, DA, AC, CB, BA, AD, DB, BC
Course 4: DB, BC, CD, DA, AC, CB, BA, AD

1 enters at A, completes his course and is joined by 3. Together they complete their courses and are joined by 4. Together all three complete their courses and are joined by 2. Together all four complete their courses. Exit 1. 2, 3 and 4 continue and complete their courses. Exit 3. 2 and 4 continue and complete their courses. Exit 4. End of 1st series. 2 continues, opening 2nd series, completes his course and is joined by 1. Etc. Unbroken movement.

1st series (as above):	1, 13, 134, 1342, 342, 42
2nd series:	2, 21, 214, 2143, 143, 43
3rd series:	3, 32, 321, 3214, 214, 14
4th series:	4, 43, 432, 4321, 321, 21

Four possible solos all given.
Six possible duos all given (two twice).
Four possible trios all given twice.

Without interruption begin repeat and fade out on 1 pacing alone. (1, 5)

Light: (2)
Dim on area from above fading out into dark.
    Four sources of differently coloured light clustered together.
    Each player has his particular light, to be turned on when he enters, kept on while he paces, turned off when he exits.
    Say 1 white, 2 yellow, 3 blue, 4 red. Then:
    1st series: white, white + blue, white + blue + red, white + blue + red + yellow, blue + red + yellow, red + yellow.
    2nd series: yellow, yellow + white, yellow + white + red etc.
    All possible light combinations given.

Percussion:
Four types of percussion, say drum, gong, triangle, wood block.
    Each player has his particular percussion, to sound when he enters, continue while he paces, cease when he exits.
    Say 1 drum, 2 gong, 3 triangle, 4 wood block. Then:
    1st series: drum, drum + triangle, drum + triangle + wood block etc. Same system as for light.
    All possible percussion combinations given.
    Percussion intermittent in all combinations to allow footsteps alone to be heard at intervals.
    Pianissimo throughout.
    Percussionists barely visible in shadow on raised podium at back of set.

Footsteps:
Each player has his particular sound.

Costumes:
Gowns reaching to ground, cowls hiding faces.

Each player has his particular colour corresponding to his light. 1 white, 2 yellow, 3 blue, 4 red.

All possible costume combinations given.

Players:
As alike in build as possible. Short and slight for preference.

Some ballet training desirable. Adolescents a possibility. Sex indifferent.

Camera:
Raised frontal. Fixed. Both players and percussionists in frame.

Time: (3)
On basis of one pace per second and allowing for time lost at angles and centre approximately 25 minutes.

Problem: (4)
Negotiation of E without rupture of rhythm when three or four players cross paths at this point. Or, if ruptures accepted, how best exploit?

(1) This original scenario (*Quad I*) was followed in the Stuttgart production by a variation (*Quad II*). (5)
(2) Abandoned as impracticable. Constant neutral light throughout.
(3) Overestimated. *Quad I*, fast tempo. 15 mins. approx. *Quad II*, slow tempo, series 1 only, 5 mins. approx.
(4) E supposed a danger zone. Hence deviation. Manoeuvre established at outset by first solo at first diagonal (CB). E.g. series 1:

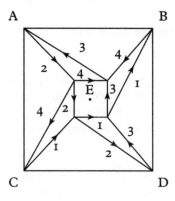

(5) No colour, all four in identical white gowns, no percussion, footsteps only sound, slow tempo, series I only.

Nacht und Träume

Written in English in 1982. First broadcast on German television (SDR) on 19 May 1983. First published by Faber and Faber and Grove Press (New York) in 1984.

Elements
  Evening light.
  Dreamer (A).
  His dreamt self (B).
  Dreamt hands R (right) and L (left).
  Last 7 bars of Schubert's *Lied, Nacht und Träume.*

1. Fade up on a dark empty room lit only by evening light
   from a window set high in back wall.
   Left foreground, faintly lit, a man seated at a table. Right
   profile, head bowed, grey hair, hands resting on table.
   Clearly visible only head and hands and section of table on
   which they rest.
2. Softly hummed, male voice, last 7 bars of Schubert's *Lied,
   Nacht und Träume.*
3. Fade out evening light.
4. Softly sung, with words, last 3 bars of *Lied* beginning
   'Holde Träume . . .'
5. Fade down A as he bows his head further to rest on hands.
   Thus minimally lit he remains just visible throughout
   dream as first viewed.
6. A dreams. Fade up on B on an invisible podium about 4 feet
   above floor level, middle ground, well right of centre. He is
   seated at a table in the same posture as A dreaming, bowed
   head resting on hands, but left profile, faintly lit by kinder
   light than A's.
7. From dark beyond and above B's head L appears and rests
   gently on it.
8. B raises his head, L withdraws and disappears.

9. From same dark R appears with a cup, conveys it gently to B's lips. B drinks, R disappears.
10. R reappears with a cloth, wipes gently B's brow, disappears with cloth.
11. B raises his head further to gaze up at invisible face.
12. B raises his right hand, still gazing up, and holds it raised palm upward.
13. R reappears and rests gently on B's right hand, B still gazing up.
14. B transfers gaze to joined hands.
15. B raises his left hand and rests it on joined hands.
16. Together hands sink to table and on them B's head.
17. L reappears and rests gently on B's head.
18. Fade out dream.
19. Fade up A and evening light.
20. A raises head to its opening position.
21. *Lied* as before (2).
22. Fade out evening light.
23. Close of *Lied* as before (4).
24. Fade down A as before (5).
25. A dreams. Fade up on B as before (6).
26. Move in slowly to close-up of B, losing A.
27. Dream as before (7–16) in close-up and slower motion.
28. Withdraw slowly to opening viewpoint, recovering A.
29. Fade out dream.
30. Fade out A.

Appendices

Appendix One

The Old Tune
A conversation piece for radio [an adaptation by
Samuel Beckett of *La Manivelle*, a play for radio by
Robert Pinget]

First broadcast on the BBC Third Programme on 23 August 1960. First published in *New Writers* 2 (John Calder Publishers, 1962).

Background of street noises. In the foreground a barrel-organ playing an old tune. 20 seconds. The mechanism jams. Thumps on the box to set it off again. No result.

GORMAN: [*Old man's cracked voice, frequent pauses for breath even in the middle of a word, speech indistinct for want of front teeth, whistling sibilants.*] There we go, bust again. [*Sound of lid raised. Scraping inside box.*] Cursed bloody music! [*Scraping. Creaking of handle. Thumps on box. The mechanism starts off again.*] Ah about time!

[*Tune resumes. 10 seconds. Sound of faltering steps approaching.*]

CREAM: [*Old man's cracked voice, stumbling speech, pauses in the middle of sentences, whistling sibilants due to ill-fitting denture.*] Well, if it isn't—[*The tune stops.*]—Gorman my old friend Gorman, do you recognize me Cream father of the judge, Cream you remember Cream.

GORMAN: Mr Cream! Well, I'll be! Mr Cream! [*Pause.*] Sit you down, sit you down, here, there. [*Pause.*] Great weather for the time of day Mr Cream, eh.

CREAM: My old friend Gorman, it's a sight to see you again after all these years, all these years.

GORMAN: Yes indeed, Mr Cream, yes indeed, that's the way it is. [*Pause.*] And you, tell me.

CREAM: I was living with my daughter and she died, then I came here to live with the other.

GORMAN: Miss Miss what?

CREAM: Bertha. You know she got married, yes, Moody the nurseryman, two children.

GORMAN: Grand match, Mr Cream, grand match, more power to you. But tell me then the poor soul she was taken then was she.

155

CREAM: Malignant, tried everything, lingered three years, that's how it goes, the young pop off and the old hang on.

GORMAN: Ah dear oh dear Mr Cream, dear oh dear.

[*Pause.*]

CREAM: And you your wife?

GORMAN: Still in it, still in it, but for how long.

CREAM: Poor Daisy yes.

GORMAN: Had she children?

CREAM: Three, three children, Johnny, the eldest, then Ronnie, then a baby girl, Queenie, my favourite, Queenie, a baby girl.

GORMAN: Darling name.

CREAM: She's so quick for her years you wouldn't believe it, do you know what she came out with to me the other day ah only the other day poor Daisy.

GORMAN: And your son-in-law?

CREAM: Eh?

GORMAN: Ah dear oh dear, Mr Cream, dear oh dear. [*Pause.*] Ah yes children that's the way it is. [*Roar of motor engine.*] They'd tear you to flitters with their flaming machines.

CREAM: Shocking crossing, sudden death.

GORMAN: As soon as look at you, tear you to flitters.

CREAM: Ah in our time Gorman this was the outskirts, you remember, peace and quiet.

GORMAN: Do I remember, fields it was, fields, bluebells, over there, on the bank, bluebells. When you think . . . [*Suddenly complete silence. 10 seconds. The tune resumes, falters, stops. Silence. The street noises resume.*] Ah the horses, the carriages, and the barouches, ah the barouches, all that's the dim distant past, Mr Cream.

CREAM: And the broughams, remember the broughams, there was style for you, the broughams.

[*Pause.*]

GORMAN: The first car I remember well I saw it here, here, on the corner, a Pic-Pic she was.

CREAM: Not a Pic-Pic, Gorman, not a Pic-Pic, a Dee Dyan Button.

GORMAN: A Pic-Pic, a Pic-Pic, don't I remember it well, just as I was coming out of Swan's the bookseller's beyond there on the corner, Swan's the bookseller's that was, just as I was coming out with a rise of fourpence ah there wasn't much money in it in those days.

CREAM: A Dee Dyan, a Dee Dyan.

GORMAN: You had to work for your living in those days, it wasn't at six you knocked off, nor at seven neither, eight it was, eight o'clock, yes by God. [*Pause.*] Where was I? [*Pause.*] Ah yes eight o'clock as I was coming out of Swan's there was the crowd gathered and the car wheeling round the bend.

CREAM: A Dee Dyan Gorman, a Dee Dyan, I can remember the man himself from Wougham he was the vintner what's this his name was.

GORMAN: Bush, Seymour Bush.

CREAM: Bush that's the man.

GORMAN: One way or t'other, Mr Cream, one way or t'other no matter it wasn't the likes of nowadays, their flaming machines they'd tear you to shreds.

CREAM: My dear Gorman do you know what it is I'm going to tell you, all this speed do you know what it is has the whole place ruinated, no living with it any more, the whole place ruinated, even the weather. [*Roar of engine.*] Ah when you think of the springs in our time remember the springs we had, the heat there was in them, and the summers remember the summers would destroy you with the heat.

GORMAN: Do I remember, there was one year back there seems like yesterday must have been round 95 when we were still out at Cruddy, didn't we water the roof of the house every evening with the rubber jet to have a bit of cool in the night, yes summer 95.

CREAM: That would surprise me Gorman, remember in those days the rubber hose was a great luxury a great luxury, wasn't till after the war the rubber hose.

GORMAN: You may be right.

CREAM: No may be about it. I tell you the first we ever had round here was in Drummond's place, old Da Drummond, that was after the war 1920 maybe, still very exorbitant it was at the time, don't you remember watering out of the can you must with that bit of garden you had didn't you, wasn't it your father owned that patch out on the Marston Road.

GORMAN: The Sheen Road Mr Cream but true for you the watering you're right there, me and me hose how are you when we had no running water at the time or had we.

CREAM: The Sheen Road, that's the one out beyond Shackleton's sawpit.

GORMAN: We didn't get it in till 1925 now it comes back to me the wash-hand basin and jug.

[*Roar of engine.*]

CREAM: The Sheen Road you saw what they've done to that I was out on it yesterday with the son-in-law, you saw what they've done to our little gardens and the grand sloe hedges.

GORMAN: Yes all those gazebos springing up like thistles there's trash for you if you like, collapse if you look at them am I right.

CREAM: Collapse is the word, when you think of the good stone made the cathedrals nothing to come up to it.

GORMAN: And on top of all no foundations, no cellars, no nothing, how are you going to live without cellars I ask you, on piles if you don't mind, piles, like in the lake age, there's progress for you.

CREAM: Ah Gorman you haven't changed a hair, just the same old wag he always was. Getting on for seventy-five is it?

GORMAN: Seventy-three, seventy-three, soon due for the knock.

CREAM: Now Gorman none of that, none of that, and me turning seventy-six, you're a young man Gorman.

GORMAN: Ah Mr Cream, always a great one for a crack.

CREAM: Here Gorman while we're at it have a fag, here. [*Pause.*] The daughter must have whipped them again, doesn't want me to be smoking, mind her own damn business. [*Pause.*] Ah I have them, here, have one.

GORMAN: I wouldn't leave you short.

CREAM: Short for God's sake, here, have one.
[*Pause.*]

GORMAN: They're packed so tight they won't come out.

CREAM: Take hold of the packet. [*Pause.*] Ah what ails me all bloody thumbs. Can you pick it up.
[*Pause.*]

GORMAN: Here we are. [*Pause.*] Ah yes a nice puff now and again but it's not what it was their gaspers now not worth a fiddler's, remember in the forces the shag remember the black shag that was tobacco for you.

CREAM: Ah the black shag my dear Gorman the black shag, fit for royalty the black shag fit for royalty. [*Pause.*] Have you a light on you.

GORMAN: Well then I haven't, the wife doesn't like me to be smoking.
[*Pause.*]

CREAM: Must have whipped my lighter too the bitch, my old tinder jizzer.

GORMAN: Well no matter I'll keep it and have a draw later on.

CREAM: The bitch sure as a gun she must have whipped it too that's going beyond the beyonds, beyond the beyonds, nothing you can call your own. [*Pause.*] Perhaps we might ask this gentleman. [*Footsteps approach.*] Beg your pardon Sir trouble you for a light.
[*Footsteps recede.*]

GORMAN: Ah the young nowadays Mr Cream very wrapped up they are the young nowadays, no thought for the old. When you think, when you think. . . . [*Suddenly complete silence. 10 seconds. The tune resumes, falters, stops. Silence. The street noises resume.*] Where were we? [*Pause.*] Ah yes the forces, you went in in 1900, 1900, 1902, am I right?

CREAM: 1903, 1903, and you 1906 was it?

GORMAN: 1906 yes at Chatham.

CREAM: The Gunners?

GORMAN: The Foot, the Foot.

CREAM: But the Foot wasn't Chatham don't you remember, there it was the Gunners, you must have been at Caterham, Caterham, the Foot.

GORMAN: Chatham I tell you, isn't it like yesterday, Morrison's pub on the corner.

CREAM: Harrison's. Harrison's Oak Lounge, do you think I don't know Chatham. I used to go there on holiday with Mrs Cream, I know Chatham backwards Gorman, inside and out, Harrison's Oak Lounge on the corner of what was the name of the street, on a rise it was, it'll come back to me, do you think I don't know Harrison's Oak Lounge there on the corner of dammit I'll forget my own name next and the square it'll come back to me.

GORMAN: Morrison or Harrison we were at Chatham.

CREAM: That would surprise me greatly, the Gunners were Chatham do you not remember that?

GORMAN: I was in the Foot, at Chatham, in the Foot.

CREAM: The Foot, that's right the Foot at Chatham.

GORMAN: That's what I'm telling you, Chatham the Foot.

CREAM: That would surprise me greatly, you must have it mucked up with the war, the mobilization.

GORMAN: The mobilization have a heart it's as clear in my mind as yesterday the mobilization, we were shifted straight away to Chesham, was it, no, Chester, that's the place, Chester, there was Morrison's pub on the corner and a chamber-maid what was her name, Joan, Jean, Jane, the very start of the war when we still didn't believe it, Chester, ah those are happy memories.

CREAM: Happy memories, happy memories, I wouldn't go so far as that.

GORMAN: I mean the start up, the start up at Chatham, we still didn't believe it, and that chamber-maid what was her name it'll come back to me. [*Pause.*] And your son by the same token.

[*Roar of engine.*]

CREAM: Eh?

GORMAN: Your son the judge.

CREAM: He has rheumatism.

GORMAN: Ah rheumatism, rheumatism runs in the blood Mr Cream.

CREAM: What are you talking about, I never had rheumatism.

GORMAN: When I think of my poor old mother, only sixty and couldn't move a muscle. [*Roar of engine.*] Rheumatism they never found the remedy for it yet, atom rockets is all they care about, I can thank my lucky stars touch wood. [*Pause.*] Your son yes he's in the papers the Carton affair, the way he managed that case he can be a proud man, the wife read it again in this morning's *Lark*.

CREAM: What do you mean the Barton affair.

GORMAN: The Carton affair Mr Cream, the sex fiend, on the Assizes.

CREAM: That's not him, he's not the Assizes my boy isn't, he's the County Courts, you mean Judge . . . Judge . . . what's this his name was in the Barton affair.

GORMAN: Ah I thought it was him.

CREAM: Certainly not I tell you, the County Courts my boy, not the Assizes, the County Courts.

GORMAN: Oh you know the Courts and the Assizes it was always all six of one to me.

CREAM: Ah but there's a big difference Mr Gorman, a power of difference, a civil case and a criminal one, quite another how d'you do, what would a civil case be doing in the *Lark* now I ask you.

GORMAN: All that machinery you know I never got the swing of it and now it's all six of one to me.

CREAM: Were you never in the Courts?

GORMAN: I was once all right when my niece got her divorce that was when was it now thirty years ago yes thirty years, I was greatly put about I can tell you the poor little thing divorced after two years of married life, my sister was never the same after it.

CREAM: Divorce is the curse of society you can take it from me, the curse of society, ask my boy if you don't believe me.

GORMAN: Ah there I'm with you the curse of society look at what it leads up to, when you think my niece had a little girl as good as never knew her father.

CREAM: Did she get alimony.

GORMAN: She was put out to board and wasted away to a shadow, that's a nice thing for you.

CREAM: Did the mother get alimony.

GORMAN: Divil the money. [*Pause.*] So that's your son ladling out the divorces.

CREAM: As a judge he must, as a father it goes to his heart.

GORMAN: Has he children.

CREAM: Well in a way he had one, little Herbert, lived to be four months then passed away, how long is it now, how long is it now.

GORMAN: Ah dear oh dear, Mr Cream, dear oh dear and did they never have another?

[*Roar of engine.*]

CREAM: Eh?

GORMAN: Other children.

CREAM: Didn't I tell you, I have my daughters' children, my two daughters. [*Pause.*] Talking of that your man there Barton the sex boyo isn't that nice carryings on for you showing himself off like that without a stitch on him to little children might just as well have been ours Gorman, our own little grandchildren.

[*Roar of engine.*]

GORMAN: Mrs Cream must be a proud woman too to be a grandmother.

CREAM: Mrs Cream is in her coffin these twenty years Mr Gorman.

GORMAN: Oh God forgive me what am I talking about, I'm getting you wouldn't know what I'd be talking about, that's right you were saying you were with Miss Daisy.

CREAM: With my daughter Bertha, Mr Gorman, my daughter Bertha, Mrs Rupert Moody.

GORMAN: Your daughter Bertha that's right so she married Moody, gallous garage they have there near the slaughter-house.

CREAM: Not him, his brother the nursery-man.

GORMAN: Grand match, more power to you, have they children?

[*Roar of engine.*]

CREAM: Eh?

GORMAN: Children.

CREAM: Two dotey little boys, little Johnny I mean Hubert and the other, the other.

GORMAN: But tell me your daughter poor soul she was taken then was she. [*Pause.*] That cigarette while we're at it might try this gentleman. [*Footsteps approach.*] Beg your pardon Sir trouble you for a light. [*Footsteps recede.*] Ah the young are very wrapped up Mr Cream.

CREAM: Little Hubert and the other, the other, what's this his name is. [*Pause.*] And Mrs Gorman.

GORMAN: Still in it.

CREAM: Ah you're the lucky jim Gorman, you're the lucky jim, Mrs Gorman by gad, fine figure of a woman Mrs Gorman, fine handsome woman.

GORMAN: Handsome, all right, but you know, age. We have our health thanks be to God touch wood. [*Pause.*] You know what it is Mr Cream, that'd be the way to pop off chatting away like this of a sunny morning.

CREAM: None of that now Gorman, who's talking of popping off with the health you have as strong as an ox and a comfortable wife, ah I'd give ten years of mine to have her back do you hear me, living with strangers isn't the same.

GORMAN: Miss Bertha's so sweet and good you're on the pig's back for God's sake, on the pig's back.

CREAM: It's not the same you can take it from me, can't call your soul your own, look at the cigarettes, the lighter.

GORMAN: Miss Bertha so sweet and good.

CREAM: Sweet and good, all right, but dammit if she doesn't take me for a doddering old drivelling dotard. [*Pause.*] What did I do with those cigarettes?

GORMAN: And tell me your poor dear daughter-in-law what am I saying your daughter-in-law.

CREAM: My daughter-in-law, my daughter-in-law, what about my daughter-in-law.

GORMAN: She had private means, it was said she had private means.

CREAM: Private means ah they were the queer private means, all swallied up in the war every ha'penny do you hear me, all in the bank the private means not as much land as you'd tether a goat. [*Pause.*] Land Gorman there's no security like land but that woman you might as well have been talking to the bedpost, a mule she was that woman was.

GORMAN: Ah well it's only human nature, you can't always pierce into the future.

CREAM: Now now Gorman don't be telling me, land wouldn't you live all your life off a bit of land damn it now wouldn't you any fool knows that unless they take the fantasy to go and build on the moon the way they say, ah that's all fantasy Gorman you can take it from me all fantasy and delusion, they'll smart for it one of these days by God they will.

GORMAN: You don't believe in the moon what they're experimenting at.

CREAM: My dear Gorman the moon is the moon and cheese is cheese what do they take us for, didn't it always exist the moon wasn't it always there as large as life and what did it ever mean only fantasy and delusion Gorman, fantasy and delusion. [*Pause.*] Or is it our forefathers were a lot of old bags maybe now is that on the cards I ask you, Bacon, Wellington, Washington, for them the moon was always in their opinion damn it I ask you you'd think to hear them talk no one ever bothered his arse with the moon before, make a cat swallow his whiskers they think they've discovered the moon as if as if. [*Pause.*] What was I driving at? [*Roar of engine.*]

GORMAN: So you're against progress are you.

CREAM: Progress, progress, progress is all very fine and grand, there's such a thing I grant you, but it's scientific, progress, scientific, the moon's not progress, lunacy, lunacy.

GORMAN: Ah there I'm with you progress is scientific and the moon, the moon, that's the way it is.

CREAM: The wisdom of the ancients that's the trouble they don't give a rap or a snap for it any more, and the world going to rack and ruin, wouldn't it be better now to go back to the old maxims and not be gallivanting off killing one another in China over the moon, ah when I think of my poor father.

GORMAN: Your father that reminds me I knew your father well. [*Roar of engine.*] There was a man for you old Mr Cream, what he had to say he lashed out with it straight from the shoulder and no humming and hawing, now it comes back to me one year there on the town council my father told me must have been wait now till I see 95, 95 or 6, a short while before he resigned, 95 that's it the year of the great frost.

CREAM: Ah I beg your pardon, the great frost was 93 I'd just turned ten, 93 Gorman the great frost. [*Roar of engine.*]

GORMAN: My father used to tell the story how Mr Cream went hell for leather for the mayor who was he in those days, must have been Overend, yes Overend.

CREAM: Ah there you're mistaken my dear Gorman, my father went on the council with Overend in 97, January 97.

GORMAN: That may be, that may be, but it must have been 95 or 6 just the same seeing as how my father went off in 96, April 96, there was a set against him and he had to give in his resignation.

CREAM: Well then your father was off when it happened, all I know is mine went on with Overend in 97 the year Marrable was burnt out.

GORMAN: Ah Marrable it wasn't five hundred yards from the door five hundred yards Mr Cream, I can still hear my poor mother saying to us ah poor dear Maria she was saying to me again only last night, January 96 that's right.

CREAM: 97 I tell you, 97, the year my father was voted on.

GORMAN: That may be but just the same the clout he gave Overend that's right now I have it.

CREAM: The clout was Oscar Bliss the butcher in Pollox Street.

GORMAN: The butcher in Pollox Street, there's a memory from the dim distant past for you, didn't he have a daughter do you remember.

CREAM: Helen, Helen Bliss, pretty girl, she'd be my age, 83 saw the light of day.

GORMAN: And Rosie Plumpton bonny Rosie staring up at the lid these thirty years she must be now and Molly Berry and Eva what was her name Eva Hart that's right Eva Hart didn't she marry a Crumplin.

CREAM: Her brother, her brother Alfred married Gertie Crumplin great one for the lads she was you remember, Gertie great one for the lads.

GORMAN: Do I remember, Gertie Crumplin great bit of skirt by God, hee hee hee great bit of skirt.

CREAM: You old dog you!

[*Roar of engine.*]

GORMAN: And Nelly Crowther there's one came to a nasty end.

CREAM: Simon's daughter that's right, the parents were greatly to blame you can take it from me.

GORMAN: They reared her well then just the same bled themselves white for her so they did, poor Mary used to tell us all we were very close in those days lived on the same landing you know, poor Mary yes she used to say what a drain it was having the child boarding out at Saint Theresa's can you imagine, very classy, daughters of the gentry Mr Cream, even taught French they were the young ladies.

CREAM: Isn't that what I'm telling you, reared her like a princess of the blood they did, French now I ask you, French.

GORMAN: Would you blame them Mr Cream, the best of parents, you can't deny it, education.

CREAM: French, French, isn't that what I'm saying.

[*Roar of engine.*]

GORMAN: They denied themselves everything, take the bits out of their mouths they would for their Nelly.

CREAM: Don't be telling me they had her on a string all the same the said young lady, remember that Holy Week 1912 was it or 13.

[*Roar of engine.*]

GORMAN: Eh?

CREAM: When you think of Simon the man he was don't be telling me that. [*Pause.*] Holy Week 1913 now it all comes back to me is that like as if they had her on a string what she did then.

GORMAN: Peace to her ashes Mr Cream.

CREAM: Principles, Gorman, principles without principles I ask you. [*Roar of engine.*] Wasn't there an army man in it.

GORMAN: Eh?

CREAM: Wasn't there an army man in it?

GORMAN: In the car?

CREAM: Eh?

GORMAN: An army man in the car?

CREAM: In the Crowther blow-up.

[*Roar of engine.*]

GORMAN: You mean the Lootnant St John Fitzball.

CREAM: St John Fitzball that's the man, wasn't he mixed up in it?

GORMAN: They were keeping company all right. [*Pause.*] He died in 14. Wounds.

CREAM: And his aunt Miss Hester.

GORMAN: Dead then these how many years is it now how many.

CREAM: She was a great old one, a little on the high and mighty side perhaps you might say.

GORMAN: Take fire like gunpowder but a heart of gold if you only knew. [*Roar of engine.*] Her niece has a chip of the old block wouldn't you say.

CREAM: Her niece? No recollection.

GORMAN: No recollection, Miss Victoria, come on now, she was to have married an American and she's in the Turrets yet.

CREAM: I thought they'd sold.

GORMAN: Sell the Turrets is it they'll never sell, the family seat three centuries and maybe more, three centuries Mr Cream.

CREAM: You might be their historiographer Gorman to hear you talk, what you don't know about those people.

GORMAN: Histryographer no Mr Cream I wouldn't go so far as that but Miss Victoria right enough I know her through and through we stop and have a gas like when her aunt was still in it, ah yes nothing hoity-toity about Miss Victoria you can take my word she has a great chip of the old block.

CREAM: Hadn't she a brother.

GORMAN: The Lootnant yes, died in 14. Wounds.

[*Deafening roar of engine.*]

CREAM: The bloody cars such a thing as a quiet chat I ask you. [*Pause.*] Well I'll be slipping along I'm holding you back from your work.

GORMAN: Slipping along what would you want slipping along and we only after meeting for once in a blue moon.

CREAM: Well then just a minute and smoke a quick one. [*Pause.*] What did I do with those cigarettes? [*Pause.*] You fire ahead don't mind me.

GORMAN: When you think, when you think . . .

[*Suddenly complete silence. 10 seconds. The tune resumes. The street noises resume and submerge tune a moment. Street noises and tune together crescendo. Tune finally rises above them triumphant.*]

Appendix Two

Notes on publication and
broadcast of individual plays

All That Fall

A play for radio

Written in English for the BBC, July–September 1956. First broadcast on the BBC Third Programme, 13 January 1957, directed by Donald McWhinnie. Duration: 69:39. Characters in italics appear in the drama but were not included in the original cast list.

Cast		*BBC (1957)*
Mrs Rooney		
(Maddy):	a lady in her seventies	Mary O'Farrell
Christy:	a carter	Allan McClelland
Mr Tyler:	a retired bill-broker	Brian O'Higgins
Mr Slocum:	Clerk of the Racecourse	Patrick Magee
Tommy:	a porter	Jack MacGowran
Mr Barrell:	a station-master	Harry Hutchinson
Miss Fitt:	a lady in her thirties	Sheila Ward
Mrs Tully:	*a female voice*	Peggy Marshall
Dolly	a small girl	(her 1 line omitted)
Mr Rooney		
(Dan):	husband of Mrs Rooney, blind	J. G. Devlin
Jerry	a small boy	Terrance Farrell
Lynch twins		

First published 1957 by Faber and Faber, London, and by Grove Press, New York. *Tous ceux qui tombent* (translated by Samuel Beckett and Robert Pinget) published March 1957 in *Les Lettres Nouvelles*. First French broadcast of *Tous ceux qui tombent* 19 December 1959, directed by Alan Trutat, with

Marise Paillet as Maddy and Roger Blin as Dan. First German broadcast of *Alle, die da fallen*, translated by Elmar and Erika Tophoven, Nordwestdeutscher Rundfunk (NWDR) 18 April 1957 (Maundy Thursday). Duration: 80 : 00. Published by Suhrkamp in 1957.

In the BBC production, the rural sounds and other sound effects are vocally generated by actors – a decision about which Beckett had reservations: 'I would have preferred true animal sounds to the BBC human imitators,' he wrote to Clas Zilliacus in 1975. 'Hinnys whinnie,' Beckett assured the Beckett Festival of Radio Plays in 1986, despite the 'hee-haw' in the BBC version of Christy's Hinny (the offspring of a male horse and a female donkey; the opposite of a mule, which brays and is the offspring of a female horse and a male donkey – and is sterile, as a hinny is not). Other sound effects are processed to skew them away from literal realism and suggest how they might be perceived by Maddy Rooney. Music from Schubert, String Quartet No. 14 'Death and the Maiden' (D810), second movement. BFRP used music from the Schubert Lied (D531), 'Der Tod und Das Mädchen' (text by Matthias Claudius). Maddy Rooney's expletive (while being extracted from the automobile), specified as 'Merde!' becomes 'Pity!' in the BBC and BFRP productions, and in the published editions (except for the Grove Press *Krapp's Last Tape and Other Dramatic Pieces* (1960) p. 49).

In 1972 Donald McWhinnie directed a new stereophonic recording of *All That Fall*, adhering insofar as possible to the original design; with J. G. Devlin again playing the role of Dan, and Mary Kean replacing the late Mary O'Farrell as Maddy, and again using actors to create the rural sounds.

Embers
A piece for radio

Written in English for the BBC, 1957–8, completed February 1959, and forwarded to the BBC with the title *Ebb*. First broadcast on the BBC Third Programme, 24 June 1959, directed by Donald McWhinnie. Duration: 44 : 38. RAI (Italian Radio) prize for radio drama, 1959 (not the same as the Prix Italia with which it has sometimes been confused).

BBC (1959)

Henry:	Jack MacGowran
Ada:	Kathleen Michael
Addie:	Kathleen Helme
Music Master/Riding Master:	Patrick Magee
Pianist	Cicely Hoye

First published in *Evergreen Review* (New York) November/December 1959. Published by Faber in *Krapp's Last Tape and Embers*, December 1959. First published by Grove Press in *Krapp's Last Tape and Other Dramatic Pieces*, 1960.

Translated into French as *Cendres* by Robert Pinget and Samuel Beckett, published in *Les Lettres Nouvelles* 36 (December 1959). First French (ORTF) broadcast 8 May 1966, directed by Jean-Jacques Vierne, with Roger Blin playing Henry, Delphine Seyrig as Ada, and Jean Martin the dancing and riding masters.

Translated into German as *Aschenglut* by Elmar and Erika Tophoven and first performed in Germany on Südwestfunk (SWDR) 6 October 1959, directed by Donald McWhinnie. Published by Suhrkamp in Samuel Beckett, *Dramatischen Dichtungen*, Bd. 2, 1964, and in a bilingual text, *Embers/Aschenglut* by Reclam (Stuttgart 1970).

The BBC production omits the following lines (restored in the BFRP production): 'Trying to toast his arse' (p. 37); the expletive, 'Christ!' from Henry's response to his father calling him a 'washout': 'Wish to Christ she had.' (p. 38) [despite the fact that, as John and Beryl Fletcher note, it comes from the Vulgate Bible: 'I wish to Christ my mother had washed me out before I was conceived.' (*Student's Guide* 131)]. Three other 'Christs' are spared, but both God and Jesus disappear from 'the child, I suppose, horrid little creature, wish to God we'd never had her. I used to walk with her in the fields, Jesus that was awful . . .' (p. 38) as does 'sulky little bastard,' from 'sulky little bastard, better off dead' (p. 39). The 'Argentine' becomes 'Venezuela' as the possible hideout for the disappeared father; and 'the Pampas' replaces 'Tibet' as a place where Henry might escape the sound of the sea. BFRP goes with Argentine and Pampas.

In the BBC production an electronically modified organ drone accompanies wave sounds for the 'sound of the sea' that haunts Henry, while the BFRP production uses the waves at Killiney beach to which Beckett directed the producers, and which do, in fact, make a kind of sucking sound as they recede amid the moving pebbles.

Rough for Radio I

Written in French (as *Esquisse radiophonique*) in late 1961, and first published in *Minuit 5*, September 1973. Subsequently published in *Pas suivi de quatre esquisses* (Paris: Éditions de Minuit 1977), with *Fragment du théâtre I & II*, and *Pochade radiophonique*. First published in English (translated by Beckett) as 'Sketch for Radio Play' in *Stereo Headphones*, no. 7 (Spring 1976). First published (as *Radio I*) in *Ends and Odds* (Grove Press 1976; Faber 1977).

Regarded by Beckett as an early and abandoned draft for the play that became *Cascando*, it has not been produced by the BBC, French or German radio, or included in BFRP. First performance Radio Netherlands (NOS) 1991, directed by Richard Rijnvos, with Michael Gouge, Joan Plowright and John Cage. Music composed by Richard Rijnvos and performed by the Ives Ensemble. Duration: 22 : 00.

Rough for Radio II

Written in French as *Pochade radiophonique*; begun January 1961(?), thus perhaps preceding *Rough for Radio I*, and published in *Minuit 16* (November 1975), where it is dated 'années 60s?'. Subsequently published in *Pas suivi de quatre esquisses* (Éditions de Minuit, 1977), with *Fragment du théâtre I & II*, and *Esquisse radiophonique*.

First broadcast on BBC Radio 3 in the author's English translation as *Rough for Radio*, 13 April 1976 (Samuel Beckett's

seventieth birthday), produced and directed by Martin Esslin.
Duration: 20:56.

BBC (1976)

Animator:	Harold Pinter
Stenographer:	Billie Whitelaw
Fox:	Patrick Magee
Dick (mute):	Michael Deacon

Beckett unequivocally vetoed the sound effects and echo of a prison torture chamber (heavy closing door, etc.) proposed for the BBC production, and was not pleased to find them used anyway. There is no identifiable acoustic location in the script.

First published (as *Radio II*) in *Ends and Odds* (Grove Press 1976, Faber 1977). German Broadcast première (as *Pochade Radiophonique*), SDR, Stuttgart, 1978. Directed by Otto Luben. Duration: 30:00. Published by Suhrkamp in *Gesammelte Werke: Hörspiel/Filme*.

Words and Music
A piece for radio

Written in English for collaboration with John Beckett, for the BBC, and completed towards the end of 1961. First published in *Evergreen Review* 27 (New York), November/December 1962. First published by Faber in March 1964 in *Play and Two Short Pieces for Radio*. First published by Grove in *Cascando and Other Short Dramatic Pieces* (1969).

First broadcast on the BBC Third Programme (with music composed and conducted by John Beckett), 13 November 1962. Directed by Michael Bakewell with Felix Felton as Croak, Patrick Magee as Joe (Words) and a twelve-musician BBC ensemble conducted by John Beckett as Bob (Music). Duration: 27:29

First German broadcast as *Worte und Musik*, with music by John Beckett (conducted by Mladen Gutesha) and text translated by Elmar and Erika Tophoven, on SDR (16 October) and NDR (20 October) 1963, directed by Imo Wilimzig with

Hans-Hermann Schaufuss as Croak and Kurt Haars as Joe (Words). Duration: 21:13. Combined with a broadcast of *Cascando*. Published in Samuel Beckett, *Dramatische Dichtungen*, Bd. 2 (Suhrkamp 1964).

First French broadcast as *Paroles et Musique* (in the author's French translation), with music (Bob) composed by Aric Dzierlatka, 5 January 1968. Roger Blin played Croak, Jacques Doucet played Joe (Words), and players from the Orchestre de la Suisse Romande conducted by Jean-Marie Auberson played Bob (Music). Duration: 34:00. First published Éditions de Minuit in 1966 in *Comédie et actes divers*, subtitled 'Piéce radiophonique'.

The late John Beckett's music for *Words and Music* was withdrawn soon after the original BBC recording and, regrettably, continues to be unavailable.

Cascando
A radio piece for music and voice

Written in French (December 1961–January 1962) in response to a request for a text from Marcel Mihalovici – whom French Radio (ORTF) had commissioned to set an original text by an author of his choosing. Subtitled 'invention radiophonique pour musique et voix'. First French broadcast with music by Mihalovici, conducted by Manuel Rosenthal. Produced by Paul Ventre and directed by Roger Blin who also played L'Ouvreur (Opener), with Jean Martin as La Voix (Voice) – on ORTF-France Culture, 13 October 1963. Duration: 28:00. First published (in French) in *L'VII* in April 1963.

First broadcast in English (in Beckett's translation) on the BBC Third Programme, with music by Marcel Mihalovici (imported from the German production), 6 October 1964. Produced and directed by Donald McWhinnie with Denys Hawthorne as Opener and Patrick Magee as Voice. Duration: 21:04. (Announced on the BBC as 'a meditation for radio by Samuel Beckett'.)

First published in English in the author's translation in *Evergreen Review* (May–June 1963). The same text subsequently

APPENDIX TWO

appears in *Cascando and Other Short Dramatic Pieces* (Grove
Press 1969). First published by Faber, March 1964, in *Play, and
two short pieces for radio* (the other being *Words and Music*). There
are a number of minor variations between this text and the text
as published in *The Collected Shorter Plays* (Faber, Grove Press
1984) and *The Complete Dramatic Works* (Faber, Grove Press
1986). The BBC production has minor divergences from both
published versions.

Translated into German by Elmar Tophoven, and first broad-
cast on 16 October 1963 on SDR and NDR (paired with *Words
and Music*). Directed by Imo Wilimzigk with music conducted by
Mladen Gutesha. Fred C. Siebeck played Opener and Robert
Michel, Voice. Duration: 19 : 00. Published in *Spectaculum: Texte
Moderner Hörspiele* (Suhrkamp 1963).

Film

Commissioned by Barney Rosset for Evergreen Theatre, New
York. Written in English, beginning in April 1963. Filmed in
New York, summer 1964. 35mm, black and white, sound film.
First shown publicly at the New York Film Festival 20 May
1965. Duration: (script) 30 : 00; (Evergreen production) 24 : 00.

Director:	Alan Schneider
Scenario:	Samuel Beckett
Cast:	Buster Keaton
Cinematographer:	Boris Kaufman
Camera (E):	Joe Coffey
Editor:	Sidney Meyers

European premiere, festivals and awards: 4 September 1965,
Venice Film Festival (Diploma di Merito). 1966: London Film
Festival (Outstanding Film of the Year), Oberhausen Film
Festival (Preis der Kurtzfilmtage), Tours Film Festival (Prix
Spécial du Jury), Sydney Film Festival, Kraków Film Festival.

First published by Faber (in *Eh Joe and Other Writings*, 1967).
Separately published as *Film by Samuel Beckett: Complete
scenario, Illustrations, Production shots*, with an essay 'On

Directing *Film*' by Alan Schneider (Grove Press 1969, Faber 1972). First published in French in the author's translation in *Film, suivi de Souffle*, (Éditions de Minuit 1972).

The screenplay has never been produced in its entirety as written. Technical difficulties made portions of the opening exterior sequences unusable and they appear in highly truncated form in the Evergreen production, retaining only the jostled 'elderly couple of shabby genteel aspect' – indispensable if only because they utter the only sound in the film (sometimes lost in copies on the mistaken assumption that it is a silent movie). The remainder of the released film adheres closely to Beckett's scenario.

A monochrome remake of *Film: A Screenplay by Samuel Beckett* was produced by the British Film Institute in 1979, directed by David Clark and featuring Max Wall (16mm, 26:00). It departs from Beckett's scenario by introducing colour, ambient sound and music.

Eh Joe
A piece for television

Written in English, April–May 1965. First broadcast on German television (in Elmar and Erika Tophoven's translation, *He Joe*), recorded 25 March – 1 April, and broadcast on Beckett's sixtieth birthday, 13 April 1966 (Süddeutscher Rundfunk, SDR). Directed by Samuel Beckett, with Deryk Mendel and Nancy Illig. Duration: 24:00.

First American broadcast, on New York educational station, WNDT (Channel 13), 18 April 1966. Directed by Alan Schneider, with George Rose and Rosemary Harris. Duration: 34:00. First British Broadcast recorded in January but not televised until 4 July 1966, BBC 2. Directed by Alan Gibson, assisted by Samuel Beckett, with Jack MacGowran (for whom the play was written) and Sian Phillips. Duration: 19:00. French broadcast première *Dis Joe* (in the author's translation), ORTF 2 February 1968. Réalisateur Michel Mitrani, with Jean-Louis Barrault and Madeliene Renaud.

First published (in the author's French translation, *Dis Joe*) in the 5–11 January 1966 issue of the Paris weekly, *Arts*. The translation contains variants not incorporated into the English production or the published English text. First published by Faber in 1967 (with 'other writings': *Act Without Words II* and *Film*). First US publication in *Evergreen Review* 62 (January 1969) and in *Cascando and Other Short Dramatic Pieces* (Grove Press 1963).

Beckett directed a second German recording of the play at SDR in January 1970, with Heinz Bennet and Irmgard Först. Beckett's revisions, either made in production or while translating the play into French, are not included in any published English text. See *Faber Companion* 164–165, Zilliacus 184–196, and Gontarski, *Theatrical Notebooks* IV 267–270.

Ghost Trio
A play for television

Written in English 1975–6 for the BBC. The title is from the colloquial name given to Beethoven's fifth piano trio (*The Ghost*) Opus 70 No. 1, excerpts from the largo of which are incorporated into the play, apparently chosen because Beethoven may have contemplated using this section for the witches' chorus in a projected opera on Shakespeare's *Macbeth* that was never written (Knowlson, *Damned to Fame* 549).

Recorded for 'The Lively Arts', BBC 2, in honour of Beckett's seventieth birthday, and first broadcast on 17 April 1977 in a programme for which Beckett chose the title 'Shades', which also included *Not I* and . . . *but the clouds* . . . Directed by Donald McWhinnie (assisted by Beckett) with Ronald Pickup as F, Billie Whitelaw as V, and Rupert Herder as the boy. Duration: 21 : 30.

First German broadcast as *Geistertrio* (translated by Elmar and Erika Tophoven), by Süddeutscher Rundfunk (SDR), recorded May 1977, and broadcast 1 November 1977 (in a programme entitled 'Schatten' with . . . *nur nach Gewölk* . . . [. . . *but the clouds* . . .] and the BBC production of *Not I*.

Directed by Samuel Beckett, with Klaus Herm as F, Irmgard Först as V, and Matthias Fell as the boy. Duration: 28:50. Published in *Quadnat Geister Trio, . . . nur Noch Gewölk . . ., Nacht und Träume* (Suhrkamp 1995).

First published in *Ends and Odds: Eight New Dramatic Pieces* (Grove Press 1976). First published in the UK in the first number of the *Journal of Beckett Studies* (1976), 'corrected (from the version in *Ends and Odds)* in the light of the BBC television recording'. First published by Faber in *Ends and Odds* in 1977, which incorporates Beckett's post-production revisions; though not passages describing F and camera contained in UoR MS 1519/1 (Gontarski, *Intent* 122, 125).

Published in French as *Trio du fantôme*, translated by Edith Fournier, in *Quad et autres pièces pour la télévision (Quad, Trio du fantôme, . . . que nuages . . ., Nacht und Träume,* Éditions de Minuit 1992). There has been no French broadcast of *Trio du fantôme.* Specified duration of shots is inconsistently adhered to in the productions Beckett directed.

. . . but the clouds . . .
A play for television

Written in English, October–November 1976, for the BBC. Recorded for 'The Lively Arts', BBC 2, in honour of Beckett's seventieth birthday, and first broadcast on 17 April 1977 in a programme for which Beckett chose the title 'Shades', which also included *Not I* and *Ghost Trio.* Directed by Donald McWhinnie, assisted by Beckett, with Ronald Pickup as M and Billie Whitelaw as W. Duration: 16:00. First published by Faber in *Ends and Odds* (1977), and subsequently by Grove Press in *Ends and Odds: Nine Dramatic Pieces* (1981).

First German Broadcast as . . . *nur nach Gewölk* . . . (trans. Elmar and Erika Tophoven), Süddeutscher Rundfunk (SDR), recorded May 1977 and broadcast 1 November 1977 (in a programme entitled 'Schatten' with *Geistertrio* and the BBC production of *Not I.* Directed by Beckett, with Klaus Herm as M and Komelia Doje as W. Duration: 17:00. Published in Samuel Beckett, *Quadrat, Geister-Trio, . . . nur noch Gewölk . . ., Nacht und Träume* (Suhrkamp 1995). Published in French (trans. Edith Fournier) as *. . . que nuages . . .* in *Quad et autres pièces pour la télévision* (Éditions de Minuit 1992). It has not been broadcast in France.

The title and the lines quoted in the play come from the conclusion of 'The Tower' by William Butler Yeats:

> Now I shall make my soul,
> Compelling it to study
> In a learned school
> Till the wreck of body,
> Slow decay of blood,
> Testy delirium
> Or dull decrepitude,
> Or what worse evil come—
> The death of friends, or death
> Of every brilliant eye
> That made a catch in the breath—
> Seem but the clouds of the sky
> When the horizon fades;
> Or a bird's sleepy cry
> Among the deepening shades.

Quad
A piece for four players, light, and percussion

Written in English in 1980–1, for Süddeutscher Rundfunk (SDR), performed by the Stuttgart Preparatory Ballet School: the production mentioned in the text in which Beckett indicates the performance variations from the original concept. First broadcast under the title *Quadrat 1 + 2* [after adding *Quad(rat) 2* to the original *Quad(rat) (1)*], on 8 October 1981, directed by Samuel Beckett. The same production, entitled simply *Quad*, was transmitted on BBC 2, on 16 December 1982. Durations: *Quad 1*: ca. 9:30. *Quad 2*: 4:00. (13:30).

Cast: 4 mimes ('not dancers'): Helfrid Foron, Juerg Hummel, Claudia Knupfer and Susanne Rehe. Percussion: Two Javanese gongs, African wood block, African talking drum, and (quoting Beckett) 'a wonderful wastebasket – from Rathmines' (a Dublin neighbourhood). Percussionists: Albrecht Schrade, Jörg Schaefer, Hans-Jochen Rubik and Gyula Racz.

First published as *Quad* in *Collected Shorter Plays* (Faber, Grove Press 1984). Collected in German as *Quadrat* in *Stücke für das Fernsehen*, translated by Elmar and Erika Tophoven (Suhrkamp 1996). Collected in French as *Quad* in *Quad et autres pièces pour la télévision*, trans. Edith Fournier (Éditions de Minuit 1992).

Nacht und Träume

Written in English for Süddeutscher Rundfunk (SDR) in 1982, and recorded in October 1983. Beckett specified that it should retain the German title of the Schubert *Lied* from which it originated (D827), the last seven bars of which are hummed then sung in the play: 'Holde Träume, kehret wieder!' ('Sweet dreams, come back again!'). First Broadcast 19 May 1983, SDR. Directed by Beckett, with Helfrid Furon (as both Dreamer and Dreamt Self), Dick Morgner and Stephan Pritz. Duration: 11:00.

First published in *Collected Shorter Plays* (Faber, Grove Press 1984). French translation by Edith Fournier first published in *Quad et autres pièces pour la télévision* (Éditions de Minuit 1992). German translation by Elmar Tophoven published in *Beckett: Szenen – Prosa – Verse* (Suhrkamp 1995).

The Old Tune

A conversation piece for radio
[an adaptation by Samuel Beckett of
La Manivelle by Robert Pinget]

First broadcast on the BBC Third Programme, 23 August 1960. Directed by Barbara Bray, with Jack MacGowran as Cream and Patrick Magee as Gorman. The old tune played by Gorman: 'The Bluebells of Scotland' (chosen by Beckett). Duration: 32 : 08. *La Manivelle* had been previously broadcast in French by the BBC on 27 July 1959.

First published in France as Robert Pinget, *La manivelle, pièce radiophonique, Texte anglais de Samuel Beckett* (bilingual text on facing pages), Éditions de Minuit, September 1960. First US publication in *Evergreen Review* (March–April 1961). First UK publication (bilingual text on facing pages) in *New Writers* 2 (John Calder Publishers 1962).

The Beckett Festival of Radio Plays

The USA national broadcast premières of Beckett's radio plays were created in The Beckett Festival of Radio Plays (BFRP) – a project originated by Martha Fehsenfeld, produced by Everett Frost and Faith Wilding (Louise Cleveland, Executive Producer, *All That Fall*) – with the plays directed by Everett Frost:

All That Fall was broadcast on 13 April 1986 (Beckett's eightieth birthday), with Billie Whitelaw as Maddy, David Warrilow as Dan, Alvin Epstein as Mr Slocum, Jerome Kilty as Christy and Mr Barrell, George Bartenieff as Mr Tyler, Susan Willis as Miss Fitt, Brad Friedman as Tommy, and Lute Ramblin' as Jerry. Duration: 84 : 50.

All that Fall was re-released in 1989, via National Public Radio (NPR) as the first programme in the complete BFRP series:

Embers: with Barry McGovern as Henry and Billie Whitelaw as Ada. Duration: 53 : 00.

Rough for Radio II: with W. Dennis Hunt (Animator), Amanda Plummer (Stenographer), Barry McGovern (Fox) and Charles Potter (Dick). Duration: 28 : 00.

Words and Music (with music by Morton Feldman): with Alvin Epstein as Croak, David Warrilow as Joe (Words) and the Bowery Ensemble conducted by Nils Vigeland as Bob (Music). Duration: 33 : 33.

Cascando (with music composed and conducted by William Kraft): with Fred Neumann as Opener and Alvin Epstein as Voice. Duration 20 : 00.

University of London Productions

Non-broadcast recordings of several of the radio plays were produced at the University of London Audio-Visual Centre by Katherine Worth and directed by David Clark:

Words and Music (1973): with music composed and conducted by Humphrey Searle, with Patrick Magee as Joe (Words), members of the London Sinfonia as Bob (Music) and Denys Hawthorne as Croak.

Embers (1975): with Patrick Magee as Henry, Elvi Hale as Ada.

Cascando (1984): with music composed and conducted by Humphrey Searle and performed by members of the City of London Sinfonia, with David Warrilow as Voice and Sean Barrett as Opener.

Recordings

Recordings of the original BBC productions of Beckett's radio plays are available from the British Library/BBC as a boxed set of four CDs (*Samuel Beckett, Works for Radio: The Original Broadcasts*, 2006), NSACD 24–27. Together with the Beckett Festival of Radio Plays and the University of London productions, they may be auditioned at: The Sound Archive of the British Library, and The Beckett International Foundation archive at the University of Reading (both by prior arrangement).

The BFRP productions may also be auditioned in the USA at: The Performing Arts Library at Lincoln Center of the New York Public Library, and The Samuel Beckett Archive at the University of Washington St Louis (both by prior arrangement).

There are, regrettably, no provisions for viewing the original productions of Beckett's teleplays.